Understanding And Educating
African-American Children

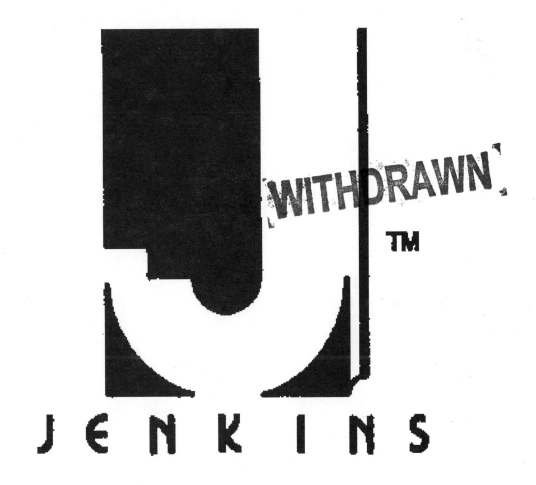

Published by William Jenkins Ent.
Copyright 1990
Reprinted: 92, 94, 96, 97,99,2000,2001

William Jenkins Ent.
P. O. Box 15134
St. Louis, MO 63110
Ph. (314)652-7944
FAX (314) 533-1850
Web Site: http://jenkins.freehosting.net
E-mail: wisdom@mo.net

PREFACE

UNDERSTANDING AND EDUCATING AFRICAN-AMERICAN CHILDREN explores and explains the multifaceted character of black children, focusing on black inner city children who present the schools with their greatest challenge. All black children are not alike and all of them do not fit the description given in these pages. But many of them are like the ones written about here, and understanding these will help the reader better understand all black children, and indeed all children.

The reader of this book should guard against seeing black people as one dimensional. Blacks have a variety of personalities, just as do other races. The essays in this book are about the different cultural and societal influences that impact black children and the variety of ways black children respond to those influences.

To the casual observer or the shallow reader, the essays may all seem to be about the same thing. But in fact, each essay is about a different dimension of the black experience and the way in which that dimension contributes to the ultimate reality of the black existence.

This is not a 'how to' book. I would not insult the intelligence of teachers by reducing their efforts to a 'one size fits all' formula. I believe that teachers are ingenious enough to take the information in this book and incorporate it into their teaching styles, curriculums, personalities, grade levels, and personal teaching situations, and be more effective in their work with children. The more we understand about how kids got to be the way they are, the more effective we can be in constructing strategies and teaching techniques to get them to where we want them to be. I hope that this book will help with that understanding and transformation.

Black children are often different, but it is not because they are black. Nothing that blacks do is done simply because they are black. Black people in America are exposed to some unique experiences, some of which were and are imposed upon them because they are black. But their responses to those experiences were and are as the responses of any people would be, given those circumstances. This book is written to help readers see the humanity of black children-to empower the reader to help black children see their own humanity, and to respond to that humanity with dignity and excellence.

ACKNOWLEDGEMENTS

I am deeply indebted to my colleagues in the teaching profession who have listened to my ideas over the years and encouraged me to make them more available to teachers across the nation.

I am grateful to my students who have valued me and constantly remind me of the important role I have played and continue to play in their lives.

I am grateful to all of my teachers who, over the years, taught me and nurtured to fruition those seeds of worth and hope that have brought me thus far.

I dedicate this book to Mrs. Naomi S. Williams, my high school English teacher, who was the first to show an interest in my writing, and has left an indelible impression for good on me for a life time; and to Dr. Richard H. Jefferson, my Humanities professor at Jackson State College, who epitomized for me what it means to be a scholar and educator; and to my mother, Mrs. Sadie L. Lloyd, who was my first and best teacher, and who still inspires me to be noble in all my endeavors.

AMBROSE T. WILLIAMS: A TRIBUTE

This book is a tribute to Mr. A. T. Williams, my high school principal, and the man to whom I owe the most for modeling for me and thousands of other young black people, what an educated black man should be. Mr. Williams was a giant in the field of education, and in the lives of the many students he touched. He set the standard for understanding and educating African-American children, a standard that I am still trying to live up to. Mr. Williams was the first principal of O'Bannon school, which was attended by children from the cotton fields of the Mississippi Delta. But during the time we were in Mr. Williams' care we were not field hands, but candidates for greatness who were guarded by his watchful eye and guided toward destinations of grandeur beyond our wildest dreams.

Mr. Williams had a vision for us and the school, and he assembled a faculty who embraced his vision of us as children with a great heritage and who would shape the future of a great race and country. He would have it no other way, and any teacher who did not share his vision for us did not work at O'Bannon school very long.

Mr. Williams was a scholar and a gentleman, who, in the loftiest of settings, never lost his common touch, always showing the highest respect for himself and others. He never even raised his voice at his teachers or his students. He was a gentleman in every aspect of his behavior.

Mr. Williams was a principal who was first and foremost, an educator, but was also an excellent administrator. With one secretary he ran a school of as many as fourteen hundred students. He coached when he needed to, drove a bus when he had to, did custodial work frequently, and on many occasions bought coats or shoes for students out of his and his wife's money. And he helped teachers and students further their education by getting scholarships for them. And when he couldn't get them scholarships, he used his own money to help them further their education.

Mr. Williams' accomplishments as principal were distinguished even more by the fact that he was the principal of an all black school that was supposedly totally controlled by whites. There were no black board members to whom he could appeal; it was only him and the white establishment. And their interests may not have been in our best interest. But Mr. Williams skillfully maneuvered his way through everything, doing almost anything he wanted to do for the good of his students. There was never any doubt about who ran O'Bannon school. O'Bannon school was Mr. Williams' school. The two were, and always will be, synonymous for those of us who attended it while he was the principal. And Mr. Williams will always be for me the epitome of what it means to be a black educator. My high regards for Mr. Williams compelled me to place this tribute to him and his work in this book. A. T. Williams was a great educator of black children. When he died, September 17,1993, he left a legacy of educational accomplishments, and hundreds of former students all over the country who credited him for any measure of success they have achieved. I join them in giving him that credit; for he certainly contributed greatly to what I am.

Table Of Contents

Table Of Contents

JENKINS

"Once you learn to read you will be forever free." Frederick Douglas

WHY I TEACH STUFF THAT SUCKS

Occasionally I will present a great idea or a great work to my students with enthusiastic anticipation, hoping for a positive response, only to have some smart mouth unabashedly proclaim, **"That sucks"**. I bolster my ego, and settle myself and respond, **"It might suck, but I'm going to teach it anyway"**. At least that is what I say verbally. My inner thoughts are, "you suck, and deserve to be taught stuff that sucks". But, of course, a class room teacher can't say things like that to students, even though students say worse things to teachers all the time.

So, I proceed, hoping he will go away. Maybe there is a cold or a bout with mono in his immediate future. But that is seldom the case. Arrogant, loud mouth students are amazingly healthy. They almost never get sick, and when they do it is usually on test day, giving the teacher the burden of giving them the test the day they return to class. Usually, however, they are there, with their smart mouth questions about the whys of such subjects as history and literature, never understanding why they should study such meaningless stuff since it has no value. And they are forever asking me why I bother to teach stuff that sucks.

Just in case this essay falls into the hands of someone who is not a teenager and has not been exposed to one in the last few years, I will explain the word 'sucks'. Teenagers today use the word 'sucks' the way teenagers used to use the word 'stinks'. What stank in the sixties sucks in the nineties. And what sucks, you may ask? Everything that kids don't like sucks. School sucks. Administrators suck. English teachers and history teachers suck. One student asked me what did Shakespeare, Milton and Chaucer have in common, and I answered that they all were great British writers. "No", he replied, "they all suck".

So, you see, 'sucks' is a word used to label all of those things that are outside of the student's pleasure interests. If it is not entertaining, pleasurable, or in some way enjoyable, it sucks. By this standard, much of what I teach in the classroom sucks. But I continue to teach it anyway. I teach it because it is an undeniable part of the whole human experience.

In spite of what my students think, human beings are not one dimensional. They are not just athletes or musicians, painters or planters. They are all of these things and more. They are multi-potential; and it is my job to keep introducing them to new things with the hope that their potential for those things will be realized and stimulated, even though many of those things suck.

I teach things that suck because I am afraid they may actually live to be adults. And if they do they will have to work, manage their money and their lives, get along with their spouses, rear and get along with their children, and participate in the democratic governmental process. And as unlikely as it seems to some of them, they are going to live to be as old as I am. And they will have to handle such personal and intimate matters as health, life and its meaning, or lack of meaning; and how they will face old age, death and dying. I fear that the information they will need to cope with these aspects of life is not being given to them in rock and rap music.

I teach stuff that sucks because I love America and what it stands for. This country promotes some beautiful principles: justice, equality, human dignity, and the eternal pursuit of the best that the human being is capable of. We need citizens who understand what America is all about and who will work to insure that every American has the opportunity to be the full recipient of all that America has to offer. The foundation of American democracy is American education. We can not have a working democracy without an educated citizenry. And democracy is the only kind of government that a truly educated citizenry will accept. A country that values democracy makes education available to all of its citizens. America has done that through the public schools. And because I love America and was educated through the public school system, I teach in that system to contribute to a process that has enriched my life.

Finally, I teach stuff that sucks because I care about the students who stink. I could not spend as much time around anyone as I spend around students without having a commitment to them. Since I have to be emotionally involved in this, I choose to do so in a loving, caring way. It may sound corny, or old fashioned, but those of us who teach, for the most part, do so because we genuinely care about and want to direct America's youth. I am no exception. I have always cared and I hope I always will. And since I care deeply about my students, I want them to have the best life that is available to them. I want them to be as happy as they can be. I teach them everything I know that I think can help them, whether it is part of the curriculum or not. I teach it in spite of the way they feel about it. I am not always right, but I always have the right thing in mind, their future and well being. And I trust that when they are older and see the value of all this stuff that I teach they will thank me because then they will see that the stuff that sucks is the stuff that saves.

"Education should focus more on where kids are going than on where they came from."
W. L. Jenkins

Teaching The Inner City Child

We have heard the expression, "all children are the same," and to a degree that statement is true. But **a child's personality and tastes are developed by the myriad of experiences he has and the impressions that go into his mind.** Those who work with children soon learn that just as they are all the same, they are also all different, and the more one knows about what makes them different the more effective that person will be in working with those children. **After years of working with black children and their families I have come to understand some of the influences in their homes, communities, and the country that make them different, especially in the way they feel about themselves, education, and America.** I share this information in the hope that teachers will use it to become more effective in teaching kids from the inner city.

These conclusions are based upon decades of living among and working with inner city children. I was a classroom teacher in the inner city of St. Louis for four years. And I have lived among the black people about whom I write for my entire life. I might add that much of my information may be more true of males than females. Because of my athletic interests during my younger years, I spent much more time around school age males than I spent around school age females. I often played ball with these young men after school and on week-ends, and during the summer. Therefore, much of my information was gathered from males. I learned about their thinking and their life styles. My observations are general, and certainly are not true about every black child from the inner city, and they are probably not true about any two to the same degree. I am not an Anthropologist. However, the observations I have made and am writing about, were carefully arrived at, and should be very helpful to those who have to teach inner city students.

I might also add that this book is written to address problems in education. Therefore, the focus is on the students who are presenting educators with the greatest problems. Needless to say, all inner city black students are not having problems in school, and the schools are not having problems with all of them. But the number of inner city black children failing in school is significant enough as to merit special attention and focus. Therefore, they are the focus of this book.

One of the first things I noticed about the inner city black child is the absence of structure in his life--at least as the middle class society would define structure. The inner city child's life does not follow the organized pattern we would like for it to follow. He is often the product of a one parent household. His home life is often loosely threaded, and there is no designation of roles and responsibilities. As a result, he is often disorganized, disoriented, and his world is usually in disarray. He shows little direction or discipline, either externally or internally.

In school this lack of structure manifests itself in bad behavior and poor study habits. Such a student often shows up in class with no paper or pen, and oftentimes without the text. When I taught in the inner city of St. Louis, teachers gave the students paper whenever writing was assigned in class. This was quite a surprise to me when I first encountered it. These same students also find it difficult to get on task and remain on task until the task is completed.

Another observation I made about the young people I encountered is that they do not understand the basic principle of our capitalist system and democratic society. The broader society runs on a reward-punishment system. This country rewards for proper behavior and punishes for improper behavior. In addition to rewarding one for proper behavior, institutions have been established at the government's expense to teach that behavior. The school, the institution established to teach proper behavior, assumes one has gotten the basics at home. That assumption is often in error when made about the black child from the inner city. It is assumed that he has learned certain basic facts about our society in his own home. In reality, he often has not. It is difficult for those who have not lived in the inner city and been exposed close up to inner city children to understand how they can be school age and know so few of the common courtesies and share so few of the common values that the rest of us take for granted. Inner city black children do not practice the kind of behavior for which the country rewards its citizens. Some do not know that behavior, others know it but arrogantly reject it.

These children are reared mostly by black women, while America, on the other hand, is run by white men. The rules that govern the lives of black women are quite different from the rules that govern the lives of white men. White men reward persons by bestowing upon them status and material things; while black women reward with love, affection and acceptance. **The white child is kept in check by his desire to share in his father's wealth.** He is schooled in this way of life very early through his allowance and through his access to the possessions his father owns. As long as he adopts the values and life style of his father, he receives the benefits a father can give. But if he rebels against his father's teachings, many of the material benefits that are given by his father are taken away until he conforms. The giving and taking of things, which is based upon approval or disapproval, is the foundation of discipline in the white community. **Discipline is simply a reason not to do something which is stronger than the desire to do it, or it is a reason to do something that is stronger than the desire not to do it. On this truth hinges all of the do's and don'ts of civilized societies, both past and present. White people tie their discipline to material rewards and require a conformity that will maintain those rewards.**

Schools are set up by a community to teach children the acceptable behavior, compiled knowledge, and inherited culture of that community so they can hold jobs and continue the life and traditions of the community. Students who do well in school are likely to do well in society. Children who understand, accept, and follow that practice, whether they agree with it or not, are generally successful. They learn to play by the rules, and are rewarded for their efforts.

Inner city blacks, on the other hand, are conditioned differently. They generally do not have much wealth. They do everything for love, affection and acceptance. Herein lies a peculiar difference between the two groups. Black women do not withhold their love, affection and acceptance from their children, regardless of what they do. Consequently, black children do not make the important connection between behavior and material rewards. They can do anything they want to do and still be loved and accepted. Consequently, they do all sorts of things, and their mothers and communities still lavish upon them affection and acceptance. **One of the reasons crime flourishes in the black community is that the people do not openly denounce and reject criminals. They often do not even report them to the police. In fact, many blacks look upon the person who tells on the criminal less favorably than they look upon the criminal himself**.

Black children from the inner city need to learn that until they adopt the behavior that the country approves of and rewards, they are wasting their time in school. It is not enough just to attend school, the student who would be successful, must attend in body, mind and spirit. It is not even enough for students just to do their work, they must do it on a standard required by the larger society. This is basic if schools are going to help black children from the inner city. **If blacks are to benefit from schools, any schools, they must gain an understanding of the system that is comparable to the understanding of those students who are successful**. Until they do, even blacks who go to suburban white schools will be going through the motions of education, but will not be preparing themselves for any of the economic benefits.

Another important consideration to be dealt with when teaching inner-city children is their value system. **Good schools work because the communities wherein they are located value education**. Successful students, for the most part, value education. Inner city students, on the other hand, often do not value it nearly as much. People do what they think they must do to get what they think they have to have. That is true with all people in every walk of life. **To change people's behavior without force, one must either change what they think they have to have, or change what they think they have to do to get it**. Children who do well in school are those who think that they can get the things that are valuable to them through education. Many inner city black children, however, don't think they can get the things they want through education.

The fact that inner city black children do not strongly believe in the merits of formal education is one thing for which they cannot be fully blamed. The country as a whole, and successful black Americans in particular who have moved out of the inner city are partly responsible. People believe what they see, if they see nothing to the contrary. **For so long black people were not properly rewarded for their educational achievements. When they started getting rewarded with good jobs, those who got the jobs often moved out of the black community, leaving behind the less well educated and the less successful. These areas that are vacated by the black middle class often become hotbeds of crime and immorality.** It is understandable how a child growing up in such an atmosphere would conclude that drug peddling and pimping were great ways to make money. He does not see many people using education as a vehicle to their dreams, so he doesn't think he can either.

Add to these conditions the fact that many poor people live in desperation. They live from **"hand to mouth"**. The things they need, they need immediately. Desperation conditions one to want everything right now; immediate gratification, immediate achievement of goals becomes the priority of the day. Education and its rewards are long-range. **It is difficult to sell a long-range goal to a child whose situation has not permitted him to look beyond the next month. Getting an education requires that one takes charge of his life**. The lives of inner city Blacks are controlled by the situation they find themselves in at any given time. They are not accustomed to taking charge of their destinies. **To get the city child to really become interested in education, two things must be done: he must first be taught to value the things education can lead to, and he must be convinced that his education will indeed lead to those things.**

Finally, I must address the teachers; the teacher must first deal with himself if he is to teach the inner city child effectively. Since many of the inner city children are now being bused to suburban schools where they are taught almost exclusively by white teachers, I feel a need to address these comments to white teachers. The teacher must be on guard against some common tendencies that white instructors have when faced with the challenge of teaching black children from the inner city.

The first and most detrimental tendency is to pity the child and relax the standards. Pity will not help city children. Black children do not need pity, they need teaching. If they are not taught to perform up to acceptable standards, they are wasting time going to good schools. Teachers should have compassion, but that compassion should lead to finding ways to help the child reach the standards rather than relaxing or lowering the standards. These high standards should definitely be maintained in the teaching of English. English teachers should teach standard English, not black dialects, not Ebonics, but standard English. And they should make no apologies for it. Black students should be required to learn and use the language properly. While they should not be put down because of their non-standard language usage, they should always be reminded of the standard and assured that in the work place standard English is what will be required of them. On standardized tests standard English is the standard. If black children are going to improve their performance on standardized tests, they must become more familiar with the language of the tests. If black children put as much time into the study of the English language as they put into the study of slang, they would be as efficient in their use of standard English as they are in their use of slang. To suggest that black children can not learn the language when others are coming from the four corners of the earth and mastering it in a year or so, is to suggest that black children are inferior to the rest of the world. If inner city black children insist on conforming to the patterns of speech that are used and known only in the black neighborhood, they are in effect limiting their success to that neighborhood.

Black children do not need to have materials watered down for them. They are just as intelligent as other children. They know just as much as white children know. It is just that much of what black children know is not valued by the rest of society. In white schools, Blacks are being challenged to learn new things, things that seem different and difficult to them. **The great challenge to teachers of black children is to find methods of introducing new material to these children in ways which will aid them in understanding and mastering that material**, and to convince black children that the rewards of mastering this challenging material is well worth the effort required to do so.

The second tendency white teachers must guard against is the tendency to retreat when accused of being racists. Black inner city children, who are often very racist themselves, are very quick to accuse white teachers of racism. Some white teachers are intimidated by such accusations and retreat in the face of them from making stringent academic or behavioral demands on black children. When the white teacher retreats, the black child wins the battle to remain undisturbed in his ways. Teachers can not afford to let that happen. They must confront the child and demand that he conforms, regardless of the child's accusations. I deal with this issue by telling students up front that most all Americans are racists. We were reared that way. Furthermore, there is nothing wrong with being a racist, if by racist you mean you make certain decisions along racial lines and expect to be buried in a cemetery where all or most of the other dead people there will be the same color you are. But I make it clear that I would never be unjust to any child because of his race, and I further state that any child who accuses me of being a racist without proper evidence is showing extreme racial prejudice himself.

I think most teachers care about their students and want them to learn, regardless of the race of the students or the teachers. I have seen very little evidence that even suggests that teachers are treating students unjustly because of their race, and I don't think this is an accusation many white teachers need to take seriously. But if a black child insists that you are a racist, tell him that surveys have indicated that some of the best teachers in the country (and indeed in the history of the world) have been racists; and assure the child that in spite of what he perceives as your racism you are going to teach him as best as you can, and that the best thing that he can do to insure that he will not become a helpless victim of mindless racism is to get the best education that is available to him, and that you are going to help him do just that.

There is also a tendency among white teachers to see themselves as inadequate in dealing with the myriad of problems the black child from the inner city brings to the class. This feeling is not unique to white teachers; concerned black teachers often feel just as inadequate. But we can not permit ourselves to be overwhelmed by that feeling. **<u>Whites must not allow themselves to conclude that because they are white they will never be able to reach black children.</u>** That is just not true. One does not have to be black to effectively teach black children, just as one does not have to be white to teach white children. White children learn from teachers of different races, why can't blacks? In almost every case I know of a black teacher teaching at a predominantly white school, that teacher is one of the favorites of the white students. If white children can reach beyond their race and embrace teachers, blacks can also. Good teachers come in all colors, and good teachers can effectively teach kids of all races. And good students of any race can learn from good teachers of any race.

Finally, white teachers must resist the notion that theirs is a missionary effort, totally charitable, with no benefits for them. Every child in this country deserves a good education. It is his entitlement; without it the constitution is simply words on paper that have no real fulfillment in his life. Black children are the descendants of proud black men and women who gave their love and their labor to make this country the great technological giant it is today. Therefore, this country has a moral obligation to educate the city child and give him a chance to be a productive and contributing citizen.

When we seriously attempt to provide that education, we will find that it will not be a one way relationship. The black man still has much to offer America. The black child has much to offer to the classroom and to the teacher. Teaching him is not a thankless chore. It can be empowering and spiritually uplifting. The city child is a survivor. In him is the embodiment of the trials and triumphs of our nation. In him are the sins and redemptions of our people. In him are the failures and the future of our humanity. In him is our hidden laughter. In him is our buried conscience. Lift him and our conscience rises with him and soars peacefully above the shame of generations past. Let him stand free and we will all walk a little taller into a future that is brighter and filled with greater promise.

"Great teachers don't just teach, they lead in the learning process; those who do not follow will not learn."   W. L. Jenkins

Factors That Hinder The Education Of Black Children In Predominantly White Schools

William Dubois said years ago that **"the problem of the twentieth century is the problem of the color line."** Even though we have made great strides in this country to erase all vestiges of racism, race is still an issue in our social fabric, and nowhere is the issue more dramatically pronounced than in our schools. Four decades after Brown v. Board of Education, black children are still the educational underclass and they are not getting a quality education, not even in white schools where more and more of them are attending. And the inner city black schools are still as deprived and dilapidated as they were before the great court decision, plus forty years of wear and tear and neglect. So those Blacks who want a better education have resorted to desegregation programs that have resulted in bussing them to predominantly white schools in white neighborhoods. Desegregated white schools have traditionally turned those Blacks who were so inclined into white prototypes who feel no responsibility for the black community, and have wedged an even deeper gap between the black poor and middle class people in America.

A critical issue in American education today is what to do with poor children, many of whom are Black, who do not subscribe to the values and goals perpetuated in our middle class oriented schools. This problem is not sufficiently addressed in our desegregated schools and Black children are the losers because of it. White schools are not serving the needs of Black children because they are incompatible with the Black child and the Black community, and they lack the knowledge, courage, and leadership to courageously address the issues that need addressing in the education of black children.

There are several factors that contribute to the incompatibility of white schools and the education of inner city black children. Combined, these factors make it difficult, if not impossible, for black children to be effectively educated at predominantly white schools, especially if those schools are not willing to make some serious adjustments.

1.   **A curriculum that is basically white European male.**

2. **A professional staff that is white and/or middle class Black and does not relate to the life styles and values of poor children, especially poor Black children.**

3. **A middle class structured school environment with rewards and punishments based solely upon middle class values.**

4. **An educational system based on theories arrived at almost exclusively by European males from their observation of European males.**

5. **A refusal to study black cultural influences as a legitimate social phenomenon that shapes Black people into cultural entities distinct from white people.**

6. **A political and school climate that would rather have peace than to address the tough issues in the education of Black children.**

7. **A faculty that does not believe strongly enough in the academic capabilities of black children, and are afraid to challenge black children to strive for excellence.**

8. **Too few black faculty to serve as mentors and leaders for black children.**

9. **A school environment that allows black children to self destruct, and then be expelled from the school.**

10. **The acceptance of black academic mediocrity and social incorrigibility as normal.**

Before I proceed with this writing, let me hasten to say that there is nothing necessarily wrong with predominantly white schools. They have worked well for white children, and the fact that they continue to send white children to some of the best schools in the world and they succeed, suggests that there is nothing wrong with the schools. The purpose of this writing is to help those schools make the kinds of adjustments that will assist black students in their attempts to succeed in such schools. And they must make these adjustments without destroying the very qualities that made them great schools in the first place.

Of all the items mentioned above, the refusal of whites to look seriously at the dynamics that impact the development of black people into cultural entities different from white people is the most crucial, and is therefore, the thrust of this effort. The others will be discussed in detail later in this book.

It annoys me when white people try to convince me that

poor white people are just like poor Black people. I don't think they mean any harm, but evidently they don't realize the gravity of the statement. Such an assertion ignores everything Blacks have experienced that is uniquely Black. It ignores our history. When I speak of history, I am not referring to slavery, although I am not excluding slavery. Such a devastating period can not be excluded from one's history. Our Black experience, however, goes back beyond slavery to the great kings of Africa, to civilizations that peaked and fell before the white European came to this continent.

I am not suggesting that the history of the Black man is a history only of great kings and sprawling civilizations. It is also a history of witch doctors and tribal leaders who were barbaric and destructive. It is a history of men and women wandering naked under the African sun, and chopping cotton in the heat of a Mississippi day. It is a history of men singing the blues in Alabama, and writing revolutionary verse in Harlem. It is a history of a people marching on Washington, and rioting in Chicago. It is the history of a people's struggle to be all that they could be in a country that insisted that they were nonentities, and could therefore be nothing without permission, a permission reluctantly granted by the 14th. amendment. All of these elements constitute the Black experience and every black person is an embodiment of every bit of that experience. **To suggest that Black is an economic condition created by the lack of money is to suggest that our history did not happen, that we arrived here just in time for the study upon which such thoughtless notions were based.**

Blackness is more than color and until the schools seriously deal with Black children as cultural entities, they are not putting forth the best efforts, nor getting the best results, from black children. **There are cultural factors that are unique to black children in America that cause many of them to tune out their formal education somewhere about the time they are making the transition from grade school to middle school.**

Many Black children make a conscious (or unconscious) decision not to do well in our middle-class oriented schools. One reason for this decision is that Black people have a national identity crisis concerning their American citizenship. **Some Blacks see themselves as Blacks who happen to be Americans, while others see themselves as Americans who happen to be black.** This may sound like a fancy play on words, but in this syntactical arrangement is the reason behind much of the problem that Blacks face in schools and in this country in general. Many Black people are confused about their dual roles as Blacks and Americans. This confusion is passed on to their children. **Around the age of 12, black children make the decision to continue, or not to continue to be successful in school, and they make this decision on the basis of their citizenship perspective.** Those who see themselves as Americans first, and then black, tie in to the system and learn the rules and pursue middle-class goals. Those who see themselves as Blacks first and Americans second, reject middle class American values and pursue their blackness. This is different from anything that any white person experiences or has experienced in America. And it is something that is not easy for a white American to understand. Granted, all children go through a stage of adjustment around the age of twelve or thirteen, but with the black child, his place in the country and his historical and community baggage, add a dimension to that adjustment that is seldom experienced by the white child.

The poorest white American should have no doubt about his citizenship and whether he belongs here. Everything around him should remind him of his place in this country. Most of the powerful figures he sees have something in common with himself, color and cultural heritage. If he has nothing it can be attributed to something he has done or is doing, and to change his fortune requires only that he changes his behavior.

Many Blacks, on the other hand, especially those who live in the inner cities of America, have tremendous doubts about their place here. They don't know whether they belong, or are accepted. And they are branded with a blackness that they can not shed. Their minds can be conditioned and reconditioned, their behavior can be refined, but their color can not be altered. They fight an enemy more powerful and permanent than poverty. They fight racism, the most degrading social sickness they will likely face.

Black children are confronted with the inferior status of Blacks in the white schools wherein they are constantly reminded of the white man's power and their own powerlessness; the white man's culture and their own cultural raping, the white man's worth and their own worthlessness. **In a more technical sense, Black children do not choose to be Black; they are forced to be Black. They operate in a school and a society that will let them be nothing else.**

They deal with their rejection by rejecting. If they can't be Americans, they can certainly be Black. They will not be black Americans, ' damn that,' they will just be

Black. They turn from white values and embrace those things they think set them apart as Black. They conform to black rhetoric. They emotionally embrace Black culture, which to them is music. They adopt Black behavior and social styles, which include dress, speech and choice of social setting. They subconsciously come to see white folks as Americans representing the American view. Since, in their minds, Whites hate them, and work diligently for their downfall, America hates them and want to see them fail.

How could one expect children with this kind of psychic make-up to function in a classroom with white children, unless such children are given special consideration when we design curriculums and formulate approaches to teaching?

There is a paranoia in Blacks about white folks that many whites would be surprised to discover. Most northern whites who have been around Blacks, have been around middle class Blacks. Middle class Blacks can present a very deceptive picture of Blacks in general, and even a deceptive picture of middle class Blacks themselves. Middle class Blacks have learned to play the game, and part of that game is to appear as they think whites want them to appear. **They understand the white mentality that says, "I will like you only if you will be like me."** But beneath the facade put up for white approval is often a far different character than what is seen by whites, a character so eloquently described in Paul Laurence Dunbar's poem, **"We Wear The Mask"**. Middle class Blacks share the culture and life styles of whites, and when whites look at them they see Black versions of themselves. Whites who know only middle class Blacks may have a very limited and distorted view of Black people in general.

Now, back to the paranoia I mentioned earlier. **Inner city Blacks are preoccupied with what they feel is a grand design on the part of whites to destroy them**. They really think that whites are out to get them. They think whites hate them and would like nothing better than to see an America rid of them. **Even middle class Blacks, many of whom have white friends who have been very loyal to them, have a deep and abiding mistrust of white people**. They see this country as one which is owned and controlled by whites, but one in which they can have a good living if they conform to the white man's expectations. The more formal education they have, the better they can do this; because formal education in America is about conformity. There is much I could say about that, but that would be another paper. I must return to this paranoia.

Because of this feeling that Blacks have about whites wanting to

destroy them, they feel a need to protect themselves from white people. Some segregate themselves into groups, some carry weapons and are ready to fight at the slightest confrontation with a white person. They often see white folks as their enemies and they approach white schools with the same attitude with which Satan approached hell in Milton's Paradise Lost: "With a mind not to be changed."

Learning, according to psychology, is change of behavior: so, if we want to educate Black children we must seek to understand them and the reasons behind their present behavior and address those reasons in order to alter that behavior, especially when they have the rights and the power to reject our instructions.

<u>**When Black children accept the notion of their Blackness, and accept along with that notion the belief that whites are out to get them, they embrace their Blackness with greater fervor**</u>. The rejection of middle class standards becomes more intense. The lower the economic status of the child, the greater the intensity of the rejection. Poorer Blacks are much more attuned to Black culture than middle class Blacks. The fact is that middle class Blacks have the flexibility to function in both cultures. The poorer Blacks, on the other hand, can fit only in the Black culture. They know this, and if they ever tried to forget it, there are a thousand things around them to remind them of their place. Their place, as they have learned from their history lessons, and from all of the indignities they have suffered and endured all over the country, is several levels lower than the lowest white American.

The frame of mind of inner city Black children must be understood if they are to be reached and challenged to grow along with their white counterparts. This understanding must become a priority of those teachers who take the teaching of Blacks seriously, and want to become successful at it. They must look at the structure of the children's environment and the structure of our schools. They must look at our educational theories and read some of the research that has been done on Black children and see how Black children differ in their development and in their attitudes, from white children. They must look at the school curriculum and see what can be done to make that curriculum more representative of our whole culture.

Finally, we must look at Black children themselves. **People are products of their environments and their environments are microcosms of their history. Tennyson said in his poem, Ulysses : "I am a part of all that I have met."** I shall add to that in reference to black children that they are also a part of all that they have heard, whether true or false. People tend to believe what they hear if they hear no contradictions. The message that black children get in the black community about America is one of confusion and distortion. It confuses them and causes them to have mixed feelings about their citizenship and their adultness.

Black boys are haunted by a particularly unique problem when making decisions about success in school. **Young black males see education as sissyish and condescending, and a denial of both their blackness and their manhood.** Since they are not given those other indicators of manhood: a job, money, authority, responsibility, and a sense of mission, this distorted manhood is all that they have. **To embrace the values promoted in the school is, to them, betrayal of their race and their manhood. No black boy worth his salt wants to turn his back on the very things that make him important.** It is easier to denounce the teachers, the school and the system than it is to denounce their budding sexuality and their cultural emergence. The challenge we face with Black boys is to get them to see that knowledge is power, and gaining control over one's own life is the most powerful and masculine thing one can do. So far, most of the white schools black boys have been attending have not met the challenge, and these boys are not being nearly as successful as they could be.

Black girls, on the other hand, are not without their problems in such schools. Since they are not as inclined to be athletes, they are not invited to join the social cliques. As a result, they create their own cliques, and more recently, with increasing frequency, gangs; thus presenting a picture of hostility and rejection to outsiders, since they see themselves as the chiefs among the rejected outsiders. Black girls need to be assured that they are valued by these predominantly white scnools and that their participation in class and the other school activities is welcomed and desired.

We are challenged to get Black boys and girls to see that this country is not out to destroy them, but would like to embrace them and give them, at last, their full citizenship; so they, and their country, can get on with the mission of making the American constitution a reality in every American's life.

Teachers and administrators at predominantly white schools can begin that process if they will look into the factors that contribute to the thinking that makes it so difficult for black children to submit themselves to the educational process and learn in our schools. By familiarizing themselves with those factors teachers can develop techniques to reach out to black children and pull them into the educational net and save them from themselves, and save them for the country.

"We shall not cease from exploring. And the end of all of our exploring shall be to end where we started, and know the place for the first time."

T. S. Elliot

The Desegregation Cycle

For the last several years I have observed first hand court-ordered desegregation. I have seen it at work across cities and from cities to counties. During the time I have observed this desegregation process I have seen some very significant and consistent trends in desegregated schools and the desegregation process. There is a pattern that they all seem to follow, and ultimately, they all end up in the same condition. These observations are not intended to alarm people, but simply to inform them. It is my hope that we can learn from the mistakes of others. Perhaps if people know about the cycles that desegregated schools go through, and know that these cycles have not had a good outcome, they will approach desegregation differently and make the process smoother and more rewarding for all involved.

First, let me describe the type of desegregated school I am speaking of: a school that has had desegregation forced upon it by the courts and the new students come mainly from communities other than the one in which the school is located. Schools in this category usually follow a trend, a trend that has led, in many cases, to a decline in the quality of education, and ultimately to the school becoming a place so absent of quality that even the people who integrated into it shun it. Nobody intends for good schools to lose their effectiveness when they become desegregated, not the new students, nor the students who have been there all the time. But it happens. It happens because people overlook some very obvious facts about people and education.

Generally, poor people have the same educational goals for their children as do wealthy people. Very few parents send their children to school to get less than the best education available to them. Often, the difference between successful students and unsuccessful ones is in the role the parents play in their children's education. **People in neighborhoods where the schools are excellent generally have a much better understanding of what makes excellent schools, and a higher level of commitment to those practices, than do those in communities that have poor schools**. People in neighborhoods where the schools are not good usually don't know what is required to have excellent schools. If they had this knowledge, and really wanted good schools, they would improve the schools in their own neighborhoods. However, they still want the best education possible for their children, even if they don't want to, or don't think they need to participate in the educational process. And when they get a chance to send their children to what they think are better schools, they jump at the opportunity.

People in poor neighborhoods with bad schools often come to some very erroneous conclusions about quality education and democracy. They conclude that excellent schools require a lot of money, and, consequently, can not exist in poor communities; and that wealthier communities have good schools because they are able to spend a lot of money on those schools. They further conclude that all their children need to do to get a good education is to enroll in one of these schools in a wealthy community. These beliefs lead to educational disaster when they are combined with the notion that in a democracy people ought to be equal, and all children ought to have equal access to the same educational opportunities, regardless of what their parents or communities are able to provide for them. Democracy and capitalism work because they allow people to be unequal; not because they require them to be equal. **When a person can only be as good as the next person, he or she loses much of the incentive for improvement**. As it is with individuals, so it is with schools. Excellent schools are excellent because the people in the communities in which they are located are willing to do the things that are necessary to have excellent schools. The residents are willing to work for and pay for that excellence. If our courts had considered this fact they might have gone about desegregation in a different manner. Instead, they have created a system and used a method which has destroyed schools and communities.

A school that has desegregation forced upon it often follows a predictable pattern. The first few outsiders come in and the local population is outraged. However, their officials and administrators at every level assure them that everything is all right. At that point in the process the officials and administrators are interested only in keeping the peace. So, in the absence of killings, stabbings, or racial confrontations, they feel victorious, and continue to assure the parents that all is well, and they chide those who express disapproval or alarm. Those who continue to sound warnings after this initial period are called "red necks" and "racists" and are henceforth ignored.

The principals are encouraged in their vigil by the first wave of new students.

These students are awed or intimidated by their new surroundings and they quietly comply. Since the first group of outside students is usually the best and the brightest, the academic difference between these new students and the indigenous population is minimal. (This fact suggests that education can take place in poor neighborhoods.) After a year these new students are claimed as the school's kids and people relax. Teachers and administrators breathe a sigh of relief and wait for the next year. In the interim they even boast about how smoothly everything went. And some of those who spoke out against the program begin to feel guilty for sounding unnecessary alarm.

The second year rolls around and more students come. The first year's process is repeated, and they get through another year rather uneventfully. By the third year, the quality of arriving students changes, little by little they are becoming a little less academically motivated and a little more inclined to cause other problems at the school. And with the presence of these less academically- motivated students the attitudes of those who were among the first to arrive change. The new students are less and less cooperative. The athletes play their sport, but will not participate in much else. The girls, for the most part, create their own groups, and the non-athletic boys spend their time trying to impress the girls. The residential students make friendly overtures to them and are rejected.

The nonresidential students are now significant enough in numbers to start recreating conditions and patterns they left in their own neighborhoods and neighborhood schools. They begin socializing almost exclusively with each other. All efforts or tendencies toward mixing with the residential population are halted, and the school begins to take on the appearance of two schools meeting in one building. And all of the problems that the non-residential students claim they left their old schools to get away from start cropping up at the new school. Incidents of fighting increase, gangs appear, and more and more of administrative time is taken up suspending and expelling this new group of students, much of it amidst charges of racism and injustices from the parents and supporters of the new group.

While this social change is going on, an academic adjustment is also being made. The new students do not have the study habits or the academic backgrounds to succeed in the regular classes, so basic classes are formed or enlarged to accommodate them. Now, they neither socialize with the residential population on their free time, nor do they take classes with them. They wind up in classes with the chronically problematic indigenous students.

While social and academic upheaval occurs, the principals are assuring everyone that things are going well. No racial fights occur, and if they do the people are told immediately that they are not racial. (After all, teenagers do have their squabbles.) After a couple of years of enlarged basic classes, someone notices that the school has become segregated socially and academically. Then, for fear of being called racists, the white well-wishers move to remedy that situation. They put more of the "busees" into the regular classes. **In order for this integration to work one of two things will have to happen: the bussed in children will have to miraculously catch up and develop new study patterns overnight, or the residential students will have to be held up until the new students catch up. What happens most frequently is obvious.**

And when it happens the standards of excellence begin to be compromised. Soon the residential students start modeling the behavior and study patterns of the new students, and what was a few years prior, an excellent school, becomes an average school.

When large numbers of basic students are dumped into regular classes, these classes become in fact basic classes; thereafter, all students who can read and write on their level will be encouraged to go into honors, lowering the standards there also.

This phenomenon, which I sometimes call in house white flight, brings us to another very important fact about a good school: someone has to exercise ownership of it. Someone has to take responsibility for it. Someone has to say: "it is mine." Interestingly enough, **an integrated school often become nobody's school**. The new students take very little responsibility for it; often considering themselves unwelcome guests. And even if they had the best of intentions, remember they came from schools that did not have what they are being asked to support at a new school. If these students had valued the attributes necessary for excellent schools, they would've developed them at their neighborhood schools, thus making the desegregation process unnecessary.

After a certain number of outsiders come in, the local residents see the school as having been taken over by the outsiders and they react accordingly. First, the most sensitive and easily disturbed pull away from the school. They stop supporting it emotionally and physically. Those who are the most affluent put their children in private schools. At first, their departure from the school is just a trickle. The departing citizens are labeled as racists by the administrators and life goes on.

In time, however, more and more people see the academic and social decline of the school and withdraw from it, taking their children with them. Now the neighborhood is ripe for starting new private schools. If no new ones are started, the attendance of existing ones swells tremendously. During this time the administrators are gloating over the great success of their extra-curricula activities. **The athletic program is usually doing better than ever, and the choir, band and drama departments flourish. Since students don't have to study, they have much more time to devote to their nonacademic skills and talents.**

After about eight years of this desegregation, people face the fact that a public school does not exist to have good ball teams or choirs; it does not exist to have a great honors program. The public school exists to educate the average child, and the majority of those children do not play ball, sing in the choir, play in the band, or act in the plays. The majority of them go to class, get a quality education and ultimately take part in running the country. The quality of a school's program can be judged by the kind of academic program it has for the average child and that is the program which suffers most when desegregation comes. That regular program is the first to go when the school begins its decline. And regardless of how much one promotes the special programs, they will not take the place of a good program for the average student.

Desegregated schools lose their average programs, everything becomes special-- which in most cases means it does not address the needs of the majority of the students. When a school reaches this stage, the parents who can, take their children out of the school, and the ones who can't, leave theirs there and hope the school does not decline further before their children graduate. The teachers who can take early retirement do, and those who have only a few years left spend more time day dreaming about retirement than they do trying to teach what they have concluded are the unteachables. By now, what was an excellent school a few years earlier, will have become a dump, despised and disowned by the people who once saw it as a proud monument to their efforts at educational excellence.

By now, everybody involved is a loser. The people in the neighborhood have lost a good school that they took pride in developing. The incoming students have lost the opportunity to get a better education than they were getting in their own neighborhood schools. The courts have lost its credibility in finding workable solutions to racial isolation and educational inequities. And the country has lost the opportunity for young citizens to get together under good circumstances and have wholesome multicultural experiences that will prepare them to live cooperatively in a culturally diverse country and world. All of the players stand empty handed when the desegregation cycle runs its course.

Not every desegregated school follows this pattern to the letter. Not every desegregation experience resembles the one I have described. And they certainly don't have to. However, many desegregated schools do follow a pattern very close to this one and do end up, after a few years, far inferior to what they were the day desegregation began. **This decline occurs especially in those schools where parents, administrators and teachers naively expect the desegregation process to work without any special efforts on their part**, or ignore the need for special interventions. Schools can take, and some have taken, steps to insure a more successful desegregation. And perhaps knowing the stages of desegregation, and having the ability to predict them, will interest and motivate more people to avert the decline and maintain excellent schools regardless of the make-up of the student body. The country is banking on the policy that blacks and whites can go to school together and those schools can be maintained as quality schools. That may not be the most ideal situation, but it is the one we have to work with now. It is in the best interest of all those connected with and served by the public schools to make public schools excellent schools. It is certainly in the best interest of black Americans whose best chance of entering the mainstream is through education, an education that most of them have access to only in the public schools. Blacks should join with other Americans and save our public schools, for by doing so, they may well be saving the only chance they have for productive citizenship in this country.

"Poverty does not cause ignorance, but ignorance almost always causes poverty."

W. L. Jenkins

Addressing The Needs of Inner City Black Students At Suburban White Schools

Education, according to our rhetoric, has become our country's top priority. Our expressed educational goal is to give each child the best education the country and his community can afford. Busing is an attempt to do that for black children from the inner city- children who, the courts say, were not getting a quality education.

Unfortunately, busing alone has not and will not solve the education problems of inner city black children, partly because of the nature of the children and partly because of the nature of the schools. We have an obligation to these children to provide for them the best educational opportunity we can afford. <u>White schools, however, have not done an effective job of educating black students from inner city black communities, partly because they have insisted on remaining all white schools</u>, and have refused to make the necessary adjustments to effectively educate black children, and partly because they have been too timid to expect and demand academic excellence and social compliance from black children. Blacks from cities have been bused into and out of predominantly white schools without getting the positive results hoped for. The schools, in effect, have not become integrated. **An integrated school is one that is attended by students who represent unrestrictedly divergent elements of the American culture and one that has a philosophy, curriculum, and programs that address with equal fervor and interests the needs of all those students**. The needs of black children have not been adequately met in white schools. In some cases, whites had no idea of what these needs were, and in others, they lacked the courage, creativity, community support, and resolve to meet those needs. However, there is still hope. And if suburban schools develop proper attitudes, programs and approaches, they could much more effectively educate black city students. But success for these students will require many adjustments from the children and the schools. And those adjustments must begin the second they enter the school building.

Establish Structure

The first thing suburban white schools should work on to more effectively educate black city children is their structure. Black city students need structure, a structure not often found at middle class suburban schools. Middle class schools have a minimum of the kind of structure that is needed by inner city black children. The relaxed middle class school environment works fine for kids who come to the school with a certain amount of internal discipline and direction, kids who have a sense of ownership in their communities and a vested interest in the well being of the community. Such kids believe that they will eventually run the institutions and businesses of their community and benefit from its bounty. Consequently, the well being of the school, which is a part of their community, is in their best interest.

Students who feel no sense of ownership do not take the same degree of responsibility for the school or for the community. Consequently, the state of the community means nothing to them since their lives will not be significantly altered by that state. Such students must have strict guidelines to adhere to until they buy into the school philosophy. These guidelines ought to include codes of conduct that are relevant, clear, widely published, and strictly enforced.

Suburban school that would effectively educate inner city children must have rules and regulations that are respected and followed by most of the students, regardless of race. Black children must be required to follow the rules. The only people our society has continually forgiven for breaking the law have been those deemed too ignorant to understand the law. Not requiring blacks to operate on an acceptable code of conduct is to suggest that they are incapable of doing so.

<u>White school officials, out of fear of racist accusations, have failed to enforce the rules on black children, and this leniency has been to the child's, school's and community's detriment.</u> Many inner city black children come from homes with very little parental authority, especially male authority. The school may be the only place between home and prison where they can learn to follow rules and deal cooperatively and effectively with authority. White schools that fail to

enforce the rules with black students are doing the students and the country a disservice. And blacks who stand in the way of white schools enforcing the school rules on black children are hurting such children rather than helping them.

Students learn better in an environment conducive to learning. Many students leave school and go to jobs or to homes that are too noisy or too crowded for study. Consequently, the school may be the only place for them to study. If the school is a place of noise, play and disorder, there might be nowhere these students can do academic work- one more reason why structure is so important.

Extending the Umbrella Of Care

Often inner city children bring many personal problems to the school, problems that beg for help as much as or more than their academic problems. They need caring adults to intervene and counsel them about sexual responsibility, moral choices and preparing for success in the business world. White schools have done little to help black students with these problems, and black people have done little to help whites feel comfortable doing so.

Effective schools depend upon educators who are not only scholars, but nurturers. Teachers in such schools provide as many or more non-academic services to students as academic ones, and these non-academic services often contribute more to a child's success than the academic ones. <u>**Good teachers are always on the look out for ways they can help their students, in class and out. They exercise ownership of these students, for they care deeply about them. But Black children from the city have not always been taken under this umbrella of care, and without this care and nurturing, much of what students need for success in life will be denied them**</u>.

Education provides information for decision making to function in one's environment. Much of this information has been given to kids in the past by their parents. **Now that many parents are unavailable to their children, large numbers of students are enrolled in our schools who wear their hats in class, use loud and abusive language in the class, the library, the halls and wherever else they find themselves when the urge strikes- students who destroy school property, steal from their classmates, carry weapons and attempt to solve**

every dispute through violence. The school can not remain silent or idle about these issues. It must either expel these children or try to reform them.

Black males are kept out of the job market or at lower levels because they are perceived to be thieves, violent, unpredictable and dangerous. That perception is not totally unfounded. Many big city newscasts mirror that image, a fact that blacks can not and should not deny. The negative image of black males can be changed by intelligent young black men living in such a way as to contradict that image and replace it with an image of young black males as intelligent, law abiding, productive citizens. **Since schools have a responsibility to prepare students for productive adult citizenship, suburban white schools should address black students in the area of their greatest need. The greatest need for many inner city children is to be brought under the umbrella of care and given the nurture and guidance needed to succeed in a society that has the cards already stacked against them, the guidance to become the kind of productive citizens that can be respected and taken seriously by the rest of society.** It is up to the schools to help produce the black citizens who will change their tarnished image.

White schools should confront these needs of their black students in a caring and effective way. They should insist that kids dress, act, and speak appropriately and they must tell them why. **A million dollar education can be wasted on a person with a fifty- cent life-style.** Schools must address the fundamental ideals by which people live their lives. And if those ideals are wrong, or inconsistent with the broader society, schools should make a serious attempt to change them. Children who do not respond and conform should be expelled from the schools. Their dismissal will be a message to them and to all students that unproductive and counter-productive behavior have no place in a civilized society. Dismissal must be carried out, and the fact that these students are black can not stand in the way of that action. **If Blacks want to go to suburban schools, believing these schools are better, they must consider why the schools are better and must not change those schools into the same kinds of ineffective schools they left.** Blacks would be ignorant to want to do that and whites would be unwise to let them. It is in the best interest of blacks that integrated schools remain quality schools. If they do not, there will be no place where the majority of black children can get a quality education. Many suburban parents can manage a private education for their children, but inner city blacks, for the most part, have only the public schools. If they lose those, they will have lost their last chance of entering into the mainstream and becoming productive citizens. If we are to save our good schools, we must address these issues immediately. We must maintain an environment conducive to learning. If we do not, very little planned learning will take place. Once we have created the proper environment, we can focus on what takes place in the classroom.

Developing the Right Attitude toward Black Children and Academics

Every teacher should approach teaching with the proper attitude, especially toward black inner city children. Teachers of these children should have the right information and the right attitude. The attitude that white teachers should bring to the classroom when teaching black children should be that black children are just as capable of learning as any other children and teachers should keep their standards and their expectations high. There is no proven inherent difference in the innate intelligence of the races. People succeed at what they work at if they work at it hard enough and long enough. Black children can be as academically successful as white children if they put the amount of interest and energy in their academic success as do the white children with whom they are being compared. Teachers generally say that they believe in the academic capabilities of black people. But many more of us believe that intellectually than do emotionally. In fact, we often do not expect black children to do as well as whites in their academic subjects. **Because blacks constantly score lower on standardized tests than whites, the conclusion has been drawn that blacks are less intelligent, thus leading many teachers to form academic prejudices against black students**.

We need to keep in mind the factors that contribute to a child's academic performance: interest and motivation, opportunity to learn, and family and community support, among other things. Another factor is the relationship between the material to be learned and the child's experiential background. Add to that complex quagmire of variables an instrument of measurement that is culturally biased, and any reasonable person could well understand why whites do better than blacks on most traditional tests. But none of the reasons have been proven to have anything to do with the intelligence of the race. With this conclusion emphatically imprinted in our minds, we can approach the teaching of Black children with high academic and social expectations. **But another major hurdle remains: what to do with kids who, because of all sorts of reasons, come to class lacking basic information that many of the other students already have-information that is vital for understanding the material on the level of instruction**. Do we lower the standards, devaluing the course for all students, teaching to the lowest; do we challenge the brightest and let the others sink or swim, teaching to the highest? Or is there a middle ground we can take? I am definitely not for either of these approaches exclusively.

We allow more time than necessary for our students to learn the material we teach. In each course there is usually enough time for review. Most high school courses can be taught in such a way that a student who is behind can make great progress and even catch up with his more advanced classmates if the teacher gives him a little extra consideration, and if the student will do a lot of extra work. The student must be challenged to do the work. The greatest burden for catching up must be placed on the person who is behind. Children who are not up to level should be told emphatically that basic material must be learned and they will not have satisfied the requirements of a course and prepared themselves to succeed at the next level until they learn that material. There are steps that teachers can take to help students who are behind.

1. **Issue at risk students two texts--one of the present course and one from a prerequisite course. Most of the principles of higher courses are explained in simpler language in texts of previous courses. Many times the material is explained in simpler terms.**

2. **Teach, rather than cover material. I find it is much more productive for students when teachers go over all of the significant material in class, even when students say they understand it.**

3. **Encourage and entertain questions. Many students would get more out of class if they would dare ask questions. Student should be led to feel that no question is too simple if it is something they don't know. Teachers can also help by trying to put themselves in `students' places and ask the questions they think they would have if the situation were reversed.**

4. **Try to keep kids focused. Make material as relevant and**

interesting as the subject will allow. Use examples that city children can relate to. Separate concepts into the individual ideas that make up the concepts.

5. Expect black children and all children to succeed and let them know they are expected to succeed.

6. Serve material in chewable chunks. Make sure students are not overwhelmed with the lesson. Give them what they can handle until they can take more. Give as many examples as possible that involve stories of people.

7. Help students get organized. Organization is very important to school success. Disorganized students waste time and energy, while organized students can get on task quicker.

8. Teach students the importance of having materials on hand.

9. Help students establish a study routine and develop the life style of a successful students.

10. Explain! Explain! Review frequently.

Aggression And Hostility

Any teacher who works with inner city children long is likely to be eventually confronted with the great hostility that many of them bring to the classroom. Some of it is racial and some of it is simply the baggage of a hostile environment. Whatever the source of this hostility, much of it is directed at the teacher. The teacher can ignore the hostile child and teach the others, the teacher can respond to the child's hostility with hostility of his or her own, or the teacher can attempt to diffuse the hostility in an effort to more effectively teach the child. But the teacher will not have much success teaching through hostility.

The teacher should not be left alone to deal with such children. They should insist that the parents get involved. The parents can be a great help here. **They should start communications with the teacher and assure the child that not only does the teacher have the child's interest at heart, but the teacher and the parents are working together in that effort.** The teacher can help by showing some interest in the child outside of the classroom. It is usually helpful for a teacher to interact with kids about their hobbies, extra-curricula activities, and even small talk about girl friends and boy friends. Once the child is convinced the teacher is genuinely interested in him he will begin to let his guards down and the hostility will diminish. Although this process can be a slow and agonizing one, it is worth the effort if the child is gained and growth occurs. I have always been helped by the fact that I was an athlete and could relate to kids who were athletes, and more and more of them are, even girls. Kids see you in a whole different light if you attend one of their athletic events. I know that all teacher don't have time to attend athletic events, but for those who do, a couple of hours in the bleachers could avoid a lot of confrontations in the classroom. It does not have to be sports, but whatever students are involved in outside of the class, teachers will gain favor with them by showing an interest in it.

Setting New Sights

Ultimately, education is a personal matter. A person is most likely to get one when he wants it; until then, any attempt at educating is usually little more than the ritual pouring of information into minds that will not retain it since they do not value it. On the contrary, when a student decides he wants to grow, when he decides he wants to elevate himself by way of his mind, very few obstacles can keep him from becoming enlightened.

Our schools need to have structure. Our teachers need the right attitude about students and their abilities. We must lower the level of hostility. But all of that will be for naught if the student does not decide that he wants an education. As difficult as the tasks I have already discussed might seem-- and they are difficult-- the task of getting black students from the city to actively pursue an education has proven to be even more difficult. Teachers of city kids are baffled at the large numbers of them who show no motivation for learning. Three reasons come to my mind immediately: education is not "cool", the rewards of it are not immediate, and the educational process is boring and difficult. But in spite of all of that, kids who want an education badly enough go after it and achieve it. We are challenged to inspire city children to aspire to an education also.

We can make them aware of the material rewards of an education and we can turn them on to the empowering quality of education. Education empowers people to be served and to serve in their communities and be honored for it. **Black children from the inner city who do not pursue education diligently aren't**

convinced of the difference education can make in their lives for the long haul. Black children, like all children, are very shortsighted. They see only the immediate future. Caring adults have to constantly remind them that time passes and life continues after one is twenty-one, and even fifty, and in most cases education prepares a person to have a better life all of his life.

Teachers can get this point across by calling attention to what has happened to people after they've passed their youth. They can remind inner city students of what has happened to outstanding college athletes who did not graduate once their playing days were over. Putting it more bluntly, they can give them a dose of reality: unless they get an education, today's glamour boys are tomorrow's bums. The teacher can also help by putting before the black student more positive role models who made it because of their minds.

The second powerful motive could be the quest for power and the desire to make a contribution to one's community and people. Kids want power. Boys particularly like to exert power and influence. This is a common need that boys have. That is why they join gangs and use violence so readily. Education is power, power for a lifetime. Many of these kids are impressed by the drug dealers they see in their neighborhoods. They are impressed by the clever people they confront on the block. They may be helped by knowing that these people are controlled by the really powerful people who used their minds rather than risked their lives on some dangerous street corner. **The people who benefit most from the corruption and the illegality in their communities are educated people-- even though their education lacks moral direction**. Black children should be directed toward the needs of the black community. White teachers can't afford to let the black child escape the needs of the community. The black community urgently needs all its people to make a contribution to it. The survival of the black community depends on that contribution.

Black children need to be given a purpose for their education. They need to be given direction toward avenues of service. Their attention needs to be called to the needs of their communities. <u>**The black boys who want only to play ball need to be reminded that athletes are in abundance in the black community, but there is a shortage of doctors, lawyers, educated civic leaders, dedicated teachers, profound and eloquent ministers, researchers, scientists and a whole array of professionals who are desperately needed by a people who have a**</u>

shortage of almost everything necessary for advancement. Kids who wear hats in class because they think it makes a black statement should be challenged to make a more powerful black statement by putting knowledge in their brains. **Kids who play around and get into trouble because they say they have nothing else to do should be reminded of how far their race has to go before they close the gap between themselves and white America on family income, life expectancy, infant mortality, and the overall quality of life.**

Black children need to be educated for so many reasons, and they are being allowed to sit around at white schools and waste time as if they owned the world, never being reminded that they are limiting themselves to a future that will give them no claim to the world except a spot to stand on some corner in a black community, a corner that will be owned by someone else.

Black children need to be confronted with the truth about the black community and the truth about themselves. The community will never be any more than they make it, and they, as black people, will never be respected as individuals at face value until the black community gains respect. This is a truth that black people can not escape and no school should allow them to hide from this truth. The great black scholars and educators of the past had missions. They had purposes for their lives, and those purposes were almost always tied to the plight of their people. We should not expect these rootless children to develop a purpose on their own apart from their people. To do so would be to expect them to do something that no other race has done.

Inspiring black students to set new sights is one of the greater challenges white schools face when teaching black children. This is the challenge they fail to accept. If they do not meet this challenge, their other efforts will be fruitless. Schools should not be left alone to motivate black children academically. Black parents, leaders, ministers, politicians, motivational speakers, and the whole nation should reach out and try to inspire black children to embrace the learning and the values that would improve their lives. **Without a meaningful mission for their education, the few black children who get one will be missionless materialists caught up in a vain search for things that will ultimately be of no service to themselves or the black community.** Of those blacks who have graduated from integrated schools and succeeded, too many of them show no active concern for the black community; a sad testimonial to integrated schools.

I have set forth what I am convinced needs to be done to address the needs of inner city black children in suburban white schools. I am the first to admit that it is not easy. I don't even know for sure whether it is possible, but I believe it is. And many of my colleagues in this profession must believe it also, for many of them, both black and white, are working diligently to make a difference in the lives of children who do not have the greatest chance with an education, but will have absolutely no chance without one.

"Ignorance is its own punishment."

W. L. Jenkins

Can The Schools Save Black Males?

The question I am posing as a title for this effort raises an even more fundamental question, a question that needs to be answered before the title question can be adequately answered. That question is, **from what do black males need to be saved?** The answer to that question, to those who are familiar with the plight of black males in this country, is rather obvious. **They need to be saved from the wasted existence many of them live their lives out in. They need to be saved from the uselessness of unemployment, and the cesspool of criminality many of them fall into. They need to be saved from the seemingly self destructive journey many of them are on. They need to be saved from the psychic horror they harbor and the mental anguish they languish in. They need to be saved from their environment and they need to be saved from themselves.**

Once we have answered that question we move to a more complicated question-**are black males worth saving?** Of course they are worth saving to their families and significant others, but are they worth saving to America? Are they worth the millions of dollars that will have to be invested in schools and the numerous professional hours that will have to go into the life of each black male to give it direction and him a chance? The answers to those questions depend upon one's perspective. **If one values the black male as an important American who deserves the assistance of other Americans, then the answer is yes.** If one values having in this country a qualified and available work force, the answer is yes. **If one values a whole America, one where every segment of the population works for the good of the entire land, and has an opportunity to benefit from the bounty of that land, the answer should be yes.**

I think that the great majority of Americans would say that all of our citizens deserve a chance to experience the ultimate in what it means to live in a democracy, to live self sufficient, self directing and self fulfilling lives. **When large segments of our population, many through no fault of their own, are trapped in** conditions that will not allow them to live productive lives, some special efforts should be mounted to remove whatever barriers that stand between these citizens and productive lives. The barriers are: racism and the remnants thereof; poverty and ignorance, apathy and addiction, and economic and social isolation. **The problems are so many and the time at school so short; what can the schools do to save people who are partially destroyed before they reach the schools? Indeed, why should the schools take on a role that is obviously not the school's responsibility?**

In fact, the school has always taken on a role with black boys that was not the responsibility of the school. **In the past, principals, male teachers, coaches and custodians have worked together to save black males from wasted lives and steered them into productive paths.** Now, with a shortage of male teachers, particularly black male teachers, and an ever shortening supply of black male principals, black boys are left with very few black positive role models at school. Consequently, the school is not as effective as it once was in directing black males.

The answer then to the question, can the schools save black males is, no! Certainly not! And educators should not allow themselves to be tricked into taking all of the responsibility for saving black males. The school can play its part if it has support from family, especially males in the family, the business community, the civic community and other institutions concerned with the development of the citizenry. The school has quite a significant role to play. **School officials and teachers need to be aware of the critical needs of the black male population.** If this awareness is felt administrators and teachers would be more likely to assist in developing programs geared at helping as many black males as possible move into productive lives. The two essays that follow are included to give teachers and school officials a better understanding of black males. It is my hope that this understanding will lead to the development of effective strategies to help those unfortunate young citizens.

THEY TELL ME I'M NO LONGER BLACK

My white friends have finally reached me.
After years of intense deprogramming
They have convinced me that I am no longer black.
I am a man, not a black man, they say.
I should not define myself on the basis of my color.
The fact that the world has done so for centuries should not matter,
According to them.
They say I am the same as other men,
The same three dollars worth of chemicals at the corner drug store.
No more, No less.
This is good news.
I no longer have to bear the awful burden of being black.
According to my white friends,
I can be free of the scars of racism and injustice.
I can now go into the streets unaware
Of the eyes of suspicion that once guarded me.
I can even stop looking forward to the revolution,
As the Jews look for the Messiah.
It, and he have come, say my Christian friends.
I no longer have to answer to a label that is synonymous with evil,
Thanks to my white friends who have saved me from such.
This should be the happiest day of my life.
This new freedom from blackness should make it so.
Somehow I don't feel this freedom as I sit here in my room
Staring at my off-white walls.
Freedom can never be extensively tested at home.
So, I must go out and find my white friends.
I will go and stand outside their country club,
And as they come out I will tell them how happy I am
That I am no longer black.
And they can tell me of all their friends at the country club that they
Have won over to their point of view.

"You will be wise to defend yourselves now, but if you let the opportunity pass, you will not be able to act even if you want to."
Demosthenes

The Role High Self Esteem Plays in the Failure of Black Males in Predominantly White Schools

For the past several years psychologists, psychiatrists, educators and social workers have talked much about self esteem and the role it plays in human behavior. Self esteem has taken the blame for many problems of the young. The chemically dependent, the teenage parent, and the high school dropout are all said to be victims of low self-esteem. And just about every problem facing black youth today has been associated, at least by some experts, with low self esteem.

I am convinced, however, that at least one problem prevalent among black males is a result of high self esteem rather than low self esteem. A case in point is the situation involving black males in predominantly white schools. **For a long time it was thought that black children who fail in these schools do so because of low self-esteem. But in many cases I have found that just the opposite is true: black boys, in particular, do not come to these schools with low self esteem; they arrive at the schools with very high self esteem (though often times they develop low self esteem after arriving).**

In the black community, black children-- particularly black male children--are regarded very highly by their family and friends. Their mothers devote much of their time and affections to these male children, misguided affections that should be extended to mature black men, but in the absence of such men, is directed to the male children. This affection contributes to the pampering of these males.

Poor black males are often shielded from the reality of their poverty by mothers who lavish upon them material things they can't afford, things that indicate an economic level way beyond the family's means. I have seen many black boys from families whose incomes were below poverty level wearing tennis shoes that cost over a hundred dollars and clothes that were more expensive than those worn by people who had many times more money. These same boys were sure that the female population of the world was waiting to be wooed by them. They had very high self esteem in their households and their neighborhoods. And the self esteem stayed in tact as long as they stayed in those communities. **The problems came, and still come, when these males venture outside of the confines of their houses and their neighborhoods**. These problems are particularly acute at predominantly white schools; for there, the differences in the things that cause one to be valued are very dramatic.

Schools generally stress skills that boys do not perform well naturally. In fact, schools stress things that few of us do well naturally. Furthermore, black boys from the city environment are less adept in the things that are valued at white schools than most of the rest of the school population, for they have spent very little time working toward excellence in the skills taught at white schools, or any schools for that matter.

White schools perpetuate middle class values, and in some instances these values are starkly different from the values of black inner city males. Chief among these difference is the way the two groups assess human worth.

Blacks have traditionally valued each other for their being. There was no price tag placed on this value. The individual did not have to do anything or accomplish anything, he just had to be. On the contrary, in the white social structure, one's worth was linked to his accomplishments. One's importance was enhanced by what he did or what he had; consequently, if a white person had five million dollars he was said to be worth five million dollars. **Since one's worth in the white community was tied to one's contribution to that community, it is understandable that a black child, coming from a community with a different approach to human worth and having nothing that the white community values, would have problems with self esteem in predominantly white schools.** When these black males face the white school and its values, they have a self esteem crisis. Their sense of worth is challenged, and often shattered by a system that devalues them because it devalues many of the things on which they have based their worth.

Their 'coolness' doesn't matter at the white school. Their jive talk is reduced to unlearned gibberish, and their expertise with the ladies becomes an exercise in childishness that they are advised to abandon in favor of a more responsible approach to male-female relationships.

Their egos are deflated and they are left frightened and lost. Their self esteem is crushed, and the more self esteem they have, the more crushing it is. Consequently, the higher the black male's self esteem is when he enters a white school, the more likely he is to fail in these schools. **It is terribly devastating when one's sense of self worth is challenged. The first tendency is to retreat into a safer and more comfortable place.** I experienced this myself when I was in college.

As a young black man I didn't like college and I told myself and everyone else who would listen that I might leave any day. I told them that I hated the standing in line and being told by others what to do, and I would put up with it no longer than the Thanksgiving holiday and then I would leave for good. I really intended not to return after the Thanksgiving holiday. That Tuesday night I packed all of my clothes into my footlocker and the next day I boarded the Greyhound bus to my hometown, Greenville, Mississippi, with the thought of not returning. It so happened that the bus went right by my grandmother's house on its way to the bus station. That evening we passed her house, the house where I lived, about sundown. As we approached and passed the house, the one with the swing on the porch, and the falling fence, and the old lady inside waiting to go home to the Jesus she had spent her life serving, I saw it and the surrounding neighborhood as I had never seen it before. **Evidently something I had learned in three months of college revealed elements of the house and the neighborhood to me that I had never noticed in the years I had lived there**. And evidently, without even knowing it, I had grown enough to fit into college even better than I could fit into that house and that neighborhood.

When I got home I never even unpacked my foot locker. That Sunday I caught the bus back to Jackson State University determined not to leave until they had conferred upon me a degree. I knew that the minor indignities I suffered there were not to be compared with the indignities I would suffer as an uneducated black man; and furthermore, I had nothing to return to. I survived that crisis, but it was not easy.

It is tough to give up comfort for struggle. One has to struggle to succeed outside of friendly environments. That is not easy. Those who do not have the fortitude to do it give up and go back where it is comfortable, especially if they are not absolutely certain that their struggle will lead to the rewards they have been promised. And since blacks, in their communities, see so little evidence of the educational struggle paying off, they are less motivated to pursue the dreams that are promised through education.

Resultingly, they return to the friendly and familiar confines of their neighborhoods, never to be heard from again-- except in a news report of a mugging, robbery or killing. They are failures by the larger society's barometer, but in their communities, for the moment at least, their egos are safe from the constant reminders of their inadequacies. And their inadequacies are real,   not just the racial concoctions of white folks.

The challenge that those of us who work with such students face is getting them beyond the initial crisis period so they can gain new skills and competencies and become valuable to the nation, thereby regaining self esteem, a wider-based self esteem that will last a life time. Our challenge is to help in that effort.

We can begin by helping these boys understand what they are experiencing and helping them to see that it is a very natural experience. The crisis they are facing and the worthlessness they are feeling is faced by and felt by almost everyone at some point in life.   That same crisis is faced by anyone who moves from a place of acceptance to one where he has to gain acceptance. It happens to every freshman who enters college. It happens to everyone who moves to a new job, a new status, or a new community. **Life imposes upon us changes that force us to, at least for a while, feel unimportant.** We all deal with this challenge, and many of us deal with it several times during our lives, **handling it better as we move from one experience to another.**

With the black male, this move is often more dramatic because of the stark contrast between what he leaves and what he encounters, both in terms of social acceptance and the differences in the way things are done in this new place. The frustration is further compounded by the pressures he often gets from those in his own community. He is often ridiculed by those left behind. This is a difficult position for children to be in, so we must always show an understanding of the situation and stress the benefits of enduring it. The difficulty of the adjustment is balanced by the rewards and the fact that one is choosing between a future of promise and one with no promise at all, except for the emptiness of acceptance for the sake of acceptance.

These black males would do well to understand that both society and they will have different expectations for them as they grow older. If they do not grow with age, if they do not develop their minds and their character, if they do not become gainfully employable and sociably acceptable in the broader society, the high esteem they have as boys is going to disappear anyway. **Those parents, girlfriends, buddies and admirers who think that as boys they are great-- with their smooth talk and smooth moves--will come to see those qualities as quite inadequate for men**. And the black males will eventually come to expect more from themselves and more out of life, but without an education they will not be able to get much more out of either. **Furthermore, even black people are becoming more materialistic, and they too are beginning to equate human worth with human productivity. And as more and more racial barriers come down, fewer racial excuses will be accepted as reasons for black failure. Expectations for black men will then be held higher by everybody. Soon there will be no place to which the black man can run to get salve for his wounded ego.**

The life of the black male who does not arrive at manhood with a clear perspective gets worse as he grows older. If he does not go to college and get into the right life style, life for him becomes a steady descent into despair. I see this despair in the faces of some of the black males who return to visit me after a few years out of school. After a taste of life beyond the comfort of the school, they understand full well the plight of black uneducated men in our society. They are then eager to help me impress upon the black males who are still in school the urgent need to take advantage of their time there and get all of the education that they can. The message to the black males must be: "You have no choice but to do it now." That choice is made more crucial by the fact that this country is much more kind to black boys than it is to black men. Every black boy will be wise to get everything society is willing to give him while he is a boy and do as much as he can with it; for when he becomes a man, many of those generous sources will dry up or be redirected to those who will still be able to be called boys. **In essence, what we are challenged to do with the black male is to get him to choose to endure now so he will have a much better life later**. This is the test of their lives for the rest of their lives. This is the period of crisis for them. This is the moment of decision. If they do not do it here and now, it will probably never be done. Every corner in the black community is a sad testimony to that truth many times over. Every unemployment office in every major city echoes it. It is a truth that rebounds off the faces of men in lines at soup kitchens and those waiting in the evenings around the doors of over-night shelters. It angrily shouts from prison cells all over the country and it whispers from graves where tombstones display dates of birth and dates of expiration too painfully close together. This is their moment; and all of us must mobilize all of our efforts and our expertise to get them to know the urgency of now and the imperative of developing new skills and new competencies for a new sense of somebodiness.

"In all things success depends upon previous preparation, and without such preparation there is sure to be failure."

Confucius

The Inner City's Black Male's Path To Failure

The plight of black males has become a topic of much discussion, and understandably so. **Black males are killing themselves and each other at a faster rate than any other group. They are filling the court dockets and prisons at a pace the country can't keep up with. They are dropping out of school in unprecedented numbers, and are more likely to be unemployed, addicted to drugs, and otherwise socially impaired than the others of our citizens. By American standards, the black male is almost certain to be condemned to a life of sub-standard existence**. In light of these facts, is it any wonder the black male is a topic of discussion.

Unfortunately, these discussions have not led to solutions. As we discuss and write about the problems of black males, the problems get worse. What is needed now is intervention. In the inner city environment black males are programmed for failure. In this environment males are conditioned to be out of step with the rest of the nation. **Once a black male stays in the inner city environment long enough to be conditioned to it, he is usually a life long social and economic cripple, unable to fit anywhere but in the wasteland in which he was bred**. If these males, born in these conditions are ever to be productive members of society they will have to be reached early and programmed for success before this programming for failure takes permanent hold. The key is intervening at the right point and basing intervention strategies upon an accurate understanding of the black male and his condition.

Several years ago I taught a sixth grade class in an all black inner city school. There were twenty-four students in the class, eleven girls and thirteen boys. It was a very good class. All of the students worked very cooperatively with me and I had good success with them. I taught these students a semester, and developed a very close bond with them during that time. I even made several trips back to visit them after I left the school, and several of them kept in touch with me throughout their high school careers.

What happened to the males in that class after sixth grade is tragic, but typical of what happens to black males in inner cities. **By the time the class reached tenth grade one of the male students was dead, another was paralyzed from a gun shot wound, three were in jail for a gang murder, and two more eventually went to prison for murdering a boy who killed one of the other boys from the class. After being such good students in sixth grade, only two of those thirteen males graduated from high school.**

What happened to those young men after sixth grade? What happens to the great majority of black males that so few of them ever lead productive lives? Why do they give up on school? Are they simply incapable of doing academic work? Is this a race of men whose plight in life is only to serve as the physical entertainment of the rest of the nation, and be forever trapped in minimum wage positions or unemployment?

Of course not! Black males can be guided into constructive and productive citizenship. The key is reaching them before they are programmed for failure, before they are turned off from education. My sixth grade boys did well in sixth grade. They were quite interested in learning and quite eager to please their teachers. At that age and stage most black boys are interested in learning and are cooperative at school. Grade school records show that there is no significant difference in the academic performance of males and females during the elementary years. It is when they pass sixth grade that there is a great decline in the academic interest and performance of black males.

The transition from sixth grade to Junior high is traumatic for children of all races of both genders. Many students of all types are lost in Junior high school. **But because of some dynamics impacting upon the lives of black people, and specifically black males, a disproportionate number of black males find the grade school to junior high transition more difficult and confusing than others, and many of them get lost during that transition and never get back on track.** An understanding by educators of how and why they go wrong is the key to enabling the schools to help black males make a successful journey into manhood.

There are four main factors that come together in the black male's life that throw him off course, and contribute to his being a failure in school and in life. Any one of these factors would slow a person down, but all of them together are just about assured to stop a person dead in

his tracks. **These factors are: <u>an inadequate and distorted definition of manhood, resulting in a self-defeating attitude toward sex and the male-female relationship; a confusion about and a preoccupation with, and allegiance to a superficial cultural blackness; a basic mistrust of American institutions and his own place in America; and the absence of a positive male</u>** authority figure in the home, leading to an undisciplined and unstructured life.**

The first factor, **the inadequate and distorted definition of manhood** begins to form very early in the inner city male's life, although it does not noticeably manifest itself until around sixth grade. <u>At about eleven years old boys begin to identify themselves more strongly as sexual beings. They become more aware of their maleness, thus becoming interested in bonding and male activities. Since they are treading new paths they look for models of manhood.</u> The kind of man a boy becomes is greatly influenced by the kind of men he sees on his way to becoming a man. **The black males, exposed only to the black community and television, get their definition of manhood mainly from that community; which consists of their peers and the males they see in that neighborhood.** Even television feeds on and projects the street image of black males. Unfortunately, the street definition of manhood which is passed on to black boys from their neighborhoods and television is quite defeating. To many of these inner city black males manhood is defined mainly in terms of sex, violence and athletics. The men they see around them boast about their sexual conquests, their athletic prowess, and their toughness, and to gain status in this fraternity of men one must be a player, a fighter or a jock, preferably all three.

To the child going through this stage; intelligence, compassion, and understanding; standard qualities of civilized behavior are seen as weaknesses. One's sexuality is more a mark of his manhood than his intelligence. And there is among these boys a crippling preoccupation with sexuality as they understand it.

Most boys are quite interested in sex in their early teens, but because of the black male's powerlessness in other areas of his life, and his lack of other wholesome activities and ways to gain self esteem, he puts more emphasis on violence, athletics and sex than do other groups of males, especially on sex. **His sexuality becomes his main focus, and he comes to see that as the central requirement of his manhood. He begins to think that sex alone makes him a man, a**

lady's man.

It is this warped sexual outlook that the inner city black male brings to his relationship with black women, an outlook that leads to a crippling relationship that is doubly damaging because of the time it comes in the male's life. This is a critical time for building the educational and social foundation he will need for the rest of his life.

At no other time will he be able to learn without cost or penalties the lessons of this period, and no other beneficial relationships will parallel the type of relationships he develops at this stage with black women. Everything he learns at this juncture that is improper will have to be unlearned later in life, at great cost to himself and society. And that which he fails to learn will have to be learned later rather painfully, or he will suffer even more pain for not knowing it.

The relationships black males develop with females at this juncture are often immature and they do not require or allow the black male to develop coping skills, and to properly mature; Consequently, there is very little learned in these relationships that can be transferred later to more wholesome relationships. In fact, they often prevent the development of such relationships.

<u>**To the black male at this stage black women are objects to be "played". They are pawns of power. The more of them the black male can claim the more powerful he is. The more he can make them do for him, (or claim they are doing for him) the more powerful still, a power he attributes almost exclusively to his sexuality. And if one of these women has his baby, that is the ultimate confirmation of his manhood, further distorting his ideas of sex and manhood. And further crippling him for his future.**</u> And since many of these males have not been around fathers who did any more than "get" them, their concept of fatherhood begins and ends with the sexual act. That is why they think they can be fathers at 16, a consensus held by most of those around them, giving impetus to their ignorance. Many of the black females with whom they enter such relationships, have no higher requirements for manhood than do the boys at this age, so they reinforce this concept. And understandably so, since all kids in their early teens think that what goes on in their homes and neighborhoods is normal, and that they are simply doing what everyone else is doing. The number of female run households, the number of black children being supported by the government rather than their fathers, and the number of teenage girls around them having babies with the approval of their parents and the rest of the community suggest to them that there is nothing wrong with that kind of life.

Black males growing up in the inner city don't know how different they are. They don't know that the world beyond their block does practically everything differently. It is traumatic when these males are confronted with the differences between their neighborhoods and the outside world, a confrontation that usually takes place first in school, which is another reason for them to reject school at that stage. School requires them to denounce what they have learned in their neighborhoods in favor of what teachers say, a task made more difficult because of the other agendas they are trying to pursue.

One of those agendas is the black male's increasing interest in a black identity. <u>**While the black male is hot in the pursuit of what he has accepted as his sexual calling, the whole dynamics of blackness is thrust upon him. Unfortunately for inner city kids, blackness for them is more a cultural fad than a philosophical stance. Just as black males in the inner city have a distorted image of manhood, they also have a distorted concept of blackness.**</u> They seldom come in contact with black men who have a profound and positive concept of their place in America, men who are comfortable with their blackness and their American citizenship, men who can serve as good examples for black males who are looking for constructive models of black manhood. There are too few such men in the inner city, so the definition of blackness that gets accepted there is the superficial one, the one that is flashy and cheaply passed from one black male to another. This image is embraced by many inner city blacks and this image continues to promote stereotypes about black males and project an anti-education or anti-refinement message.

<u>**These males do not know that the image they are so proud of projecting at that point in their lives will condemn them to a life of second class citizenship for the rest of their lives, particularly since it is counter-productive to the main goal of education, which is to assimilate into the mainstream.**</u> This goal is very difficult to accomplish with these black males while they are pursuing a black identity that requires them to stand out. While in pursuit of this black identity the black male sees cooperating with the system as a kind of submissive compliance to the system, a selling out, if you will. He, therefore, becomes very uncooperative to the organized system of behavior. He sees the school as an arm of the system, and cooperation with the school as a threat to his black identity. **To do what the school demands is to become a wimp, thus contradicting his concept of his black manhood, which requires him to be strong and do**

his own thing, while at the same time the people in the school are telling him to be compliant and cooperative.

The black male does not understand at this age how he can express his new interest in his black identity within the guidelines of acceptable middle class behavior, and at the same time pursue an education that will help him gain entrance into the middle class. He thinks, at this age, that he must choose between one or the other. If he chooses education he becomes an outcast to his peers, and if he chooses to identify with those peers he becomes a social cripple, condemned to failure everywhere except in the black community, and eventually, even there. Few outsiders know or understand the pressures inner city black males are under to conform to the inner city norm of rebellion against educational conformity. It takes a very strong person to stand alone at this time under such pressure. This situation gives meaning to Ibsen's statement in "Enemy of The People": **"The strongest man in the world is he who stands most alone."**

It is difficult for a child of twelve or thirteen to understand these sexual and social changes on his own, and since so few of the adults with whom he comes in contact in school or elsewhere understand the changes going on in his life, very few people are in a position to help him. The black male usually has to live and learn, and for him that often means gaining knowledge long after the time he is able to benefit from it, and he is not very interested in this type of knowledge at this age anyway. <u>At this age being black is what matters. It matters more than an education. It matters more than being accepted by whites. The acceptance he wants at this time in his life is from his peers, and that is gained more from wearing gold chains and ear rings than from making good grades in school and acting and talking like white folks.</u>

The inner city black male's plight is made even worse by the fact that he has a terrible distrust of the institutions in America. He doesn't feel these institutions have his best interest at heart, not even the institutions of learning. He mistrusts the police, the court system, the government, big business and anything that is controlled by whites. Because of their mistrust of American institutions black males do not believe that these institutions will work for them. When students want material things and do not pursue an education it is often because they do not believe that education will lead to the material things they want. Consequently, they devise their own methods of attaining the good life. These methods often mean a rejection of the legally prescribed path and the adoption of a criminal path. Crime is tolerated in the black community partly because black people in these communities sympathize with black law breakers under the notion that they are discriminated against and kept from achieving their goals through law abiding means, therefore, crime is the only way they can have the material things they want and somehow deserve.

White people are shocked when they hear of the number of young black men in this country who are in prison or have prison records. When one loses faith in his institutions and accepts the notion that the only way he can have anything is to take it or steal it, and he's tougher than the ones who have the things he wants, prison is where he winds up. This is not to offer any excuses for those blacks who choose crime because they prefer crime over work. There are some of those in every race. This is simply to explain one of the influences that causes black males, who would otherwise be law abiding citizens, to choose a path of crime rather than a path of compliance. This is why they don't embrace education, they don't believe it pays. They don't trust that the promises made to other Americans extend to them. They think that somehow they are going to be the victims of some white conspiracy. One has to live around black city kids to understand how deeply this mistrust goes and how crucially it affects their behavior in all things relating to the system. Black inner city children have some examples of racism and exploitation that they use to justify in their minds their mistrust of the country. But in many cases they are living in the past, a past that is affecting their futures in a very costly fashion.   Successful blacks who have proven through their own success that blacks can succeed in America by the same methods and ethics that the whites have used, are silent in conveying this message to blacks. Successful blacks too often criticize America in the presence of poor blacks in order to gain their approval and support. In the end, however, such blacks and their criticisms of America, only serve to strengthen in poor blacks the false notions that are keeping them from trusting the country and moving up.

As if confusion about his sexuality and his country were not enough to condemn any child to failure, the black child in the inner city has even another negative working against him. This period of growth, change and challenge is a terribly turbulent time in the lives of black males. It is a challenge even for those kids who have the best male role models, it is devastating for those who have none or bad ones. **Therefore the fact that the majority of inner city males have no father in the home further decreases their chances of ever fitting in**. At this time black males need firm demands placed upon them by strong and caring adult males. Boys, during this stage, will test authority. And if there is no male authority figure in the house after a year or two of confrontation with his mother, he becomes the head of the house. He is the strongest, baddest person there. The presence of a male authority figure for males is crucial at this time. The cooperation he would learn from working with authority, the discipline he would develop from having restraints placed on him is all missed. **<u>At this point school is the last thing on his mind. His image, his sex life, his financial status, his standing with his peers, his black identity, all take precedence over school. And since he has no one to call his hand, his powers go unchallenged until he comes in contact with the law</u>**. By now he has usually developed a very negative and unrealistic attitude toward authority. He has learned from his mother that he can push everyone around, and he has come to believe that there are no absolutes. **Absolutes need force to back them. Women, who do not have the force, negotiate and compromise with their sons. Unfortunately for the sons, beyond the walls of mother's house, there are absolutes. Some things are absolutely unacceptable and no amount of negotiating and compromising will get one out of them. Black males who do not learn this at home often find it out after they are behind bars facing the prospect of spending most of their lives in prison.**

Presently, in many of our northern states there are more black men in the state's prisons than there are in the state's institutions of higher learning, a sad statistic for the black community and the country. No race can improve its status in this land when the vast majority of its men lead wasteful, useless, and destructive lives. And no country can afford to allow a race of men to come up in its midst simply to imprison them for most of their adult lives.

Another unfortunate result of female run households is that the males emerge from them ill-equipped to work effectively with men. The message the black male gets about the world from his mother and girlfriend further alienate him from the social norms of the rest of the country. In confrontations with his mother and girlfriend he always wins, they back down. He gathers from these confrontations that the opposition always backs down. Resultingly, he does not learn how to resolve differences in a peaceful, fair manner. He puts his body on the line in all of his conflicts. And when the conflict is with another male, conditioned as he has been conditioned, the consequences are violent and tragic. That is one of the reasons there is such a high homicide rate among black males. Black males have not learned to compromise and negotiate their differences. In their dealing with the women in their lives, the women always back down.

If he had the opportunity to interact with a strong, fair, male, the black male would learn that one can't win all confrontations; and would then learn how to settle differences without violence. He would also learn that one can't always have everything he wants when he wants it. The things education offers, one has to wait on. Those who are not conditioned to wait are usually impulsive, and demand all things immediately, which is part of the conditioning for failure that the black child undergoes.

Probably the most crucial disadvantage of not having an adult male in the home is that boys in such homes are left with no responsible, adult male leadership. Very few of us are able to chart our own paths without guidance from others. Most of us need models. We need someone to have gone there before, and done that before. Regardless of how much young people claim they want to do their own thing, the truth is that they are looking for direction. The path from childhood to manhood is a tricky and treacherous one, if there is no one to lead the way, boys get lost, and sometimes never find their way back to the proper path.

In my teaching I have found that the males who have been the most successful in my classes have been those who chose to follow my lead. The biggest tragedy of a man leaving his children may not be that he is not there to feed them, but that he is not there to lead them. The government can feed poor children, but the government has not figured out how to lead them. Therefore, boys without fathers in the home, may have full stomachs, but empty heads, void of any sense of direction. It is easy and natural for such boys to get on a path to failure.

Consider now, such a black male in the inner city. His concept of manhood is totally out of step with society. He wants to play sports or play women to success. He wants to pursue his black identity in a way that offends his countrymen who control him from cradle to grave. He has a grave mistrust of all the institutions designed to guide him, help him, and reward him; so he chooses a path contrary to the one laid out for him by those who know the way. He has no father to provide for him, protect him, caution him, discipline him, lead him, or love him. And there he stands, alone against the world, surrounded only by an angry army of helpless creatures such as himself. There he stands: to some an object of pity, to some an object of hatred, and to some an object of shame, but

to all an enigmatic symbol of the shortcomings, complexity and difficulty of the American democratic experience. This is the black inner city male. This is what he becomes after a few years in the inner city. This is what the schools are challenged to work with.

Because of the critical situation he is in, the schools and other institutions that work with black males look for ways to intervene and salvage them. Too often, however, by the time these institutions get involved, the lives of these black males are already ruined beyond repair. And just as often **the people who are trying to intervene don't know enough about the thinking of black males to begin to straighten them out.** They don't know enough about the dynamics that make the black male what he is. In short, they don't know what makes a black man black. Consequently, school officials all across America are confused about what to do with the black male. Nothing seems to be working.

Our programs for the black male have not worked because they were void of any understanding of the black male's condition and conditioning. Little study has been done on the environment these males live in. Even blacks who have not lived in or had social contact with the inner city black child of the last twenty years, know next to nothing about such children. The black children I encounter in the inner city today are extremely different from the kids of my teenage years. Their views about life, social class, upward mobility, and even about America are different. Any program or strategy designed for these males must take into account how they think and what they value. We have been working with the black male out of a background of ignorance. We couldn't help him because we didn't understand him. We couldn't straighten him out because we did not know where he had gone wrong. Now that we have some knowledge of him, we can develop some strategies to help him.

If one wishes to take something apart without breaking it, it is essential to know how it was assembled. Knowing how the black male has developed his thinking is essential in changing that thinking and preventing such patterns in the future. Early in grade school black males should be taught the appropriate role for men in our society. They should have manhood defined in a way that is productive and rewarding. There are many ways this can be done and good teachers will find these ways when they know the need exists. Educators must counteract the inner city's model of manhood with an American model, a model that is acceptable to the country and worthy of emulating. This can be done by conscientious teachers, either in the regular classes, or in special classes designed specifically for that purpose. This will be more difficult at integrated schools, but if these schools want to reach black males, this is the concession that will have to be made. They should keep in mind that many of the models for manhood should be black. But they all do not have to be black. Black children must get beyond their color to their humanity. And they should never let their color keep them from experiencing the fullness of their humanity. Children must see themselves as capable of emulating the best models set before them. We have known for some time the value of positive role models. We simply need to implement this awareness more vigorously with the black male.

As we fashion a positive image of manhood in the mind of the black male, we must stress a wholesome, healthy relationship with females, a relationship based upon a proper attitude toward sex and sexual responsibility. In the past we have assumed that this teaching would take place in the home. Now that we know it doesn't, we must do it in school if we want to reach the students who are hampered because they don't have it.

This teaching about wholesome relationships must involve females as well as males. Black males, like other males, value their relationships with females. Black women must be taught to expect and demand more from black men. They must be taught that they deserve men who are well educated and have something to offer them other than romance. **The sympathy the black woman once showed to the black man because of his disadvantage in America is now manifesting itself in a total lack of demand on the part of black women. Consequently, some black women will accept anything from a black man. This is not good for the man or the woman, and it is not good for the black race.** I am continually baffled by black women who allow themselves to become pregnant time and time again by men who are uneducated and unlikely to ever be very successful. Such women condemn themselves and their children to a life of poverty, and the inner city black community will not improve until this demeaning cycle is broken.

Black women have also a sexual fascination with rugged, rebellious, athletic and uneducated black men. Consequently, they don't encourage their boyfriends to study; and don't show much interest in males who pursue the middle class path toward success. These women, in ways they are not aware of, encourage the very behavior they are later victimized by. Black girls need structured training and modeling in healthy and productive relationships. They need to be taught to support the behavior in men that is going to produce the type of men who will be responsible heads of black households. Schools can help raise black women's opinions of themselves and help raise their level of expectation for the men with whom they get involved, particularly those they allow to become the fathers of their children.

Beyond these two factors we must move to help the black male feel at home in America and help him feel that the American dream extends to him. Since we know that black males don't trust the system, we must counteract that by getting the institutions to respond to the needs of these males. We must get black businesses to get involved in schools and assure kids that there will be jobs awaiting them when they adequately prepare for those jobs. Contact with business leaders will help these students understand the needs and requirements of business. And they can come to understand how they fit into the plans of business. And they will discover that many blacks already have the kinds of jobs that they thought only white people could have. There are dozens of ways to approach this problem, but we must have our black males know that they are valuable to the nation, and that there is not only a place for them in this country, but a need for them.

The last factor in the black child's conditioning for failure, the absence of a male authority figure in the home, poses a greater challenge for the school than either of the other three. We can not instantly change the make-up of the black family. We can not restore black men immediately to their proper roles as heads of households in the black community; but we can use all of the male figures in our schools to guide male students. We can bring grade school boys in contact with more men. The men on our faculties and staff can spend time with black males and make a concerted effort to mold them into proper citizens, and provide them with the leadership they need. If we do this and succeed we will assure that future generations of teachers will have an easier time at this than we are having. Hopefully, many of the young men we will help will shed, or avoid altogether, this loser conditioning, and be winners and head households wherein future black boys will be reared, boys that will be whole and at peace with themselves and society. This is a great challenge that calls the schools to another level of service. It is asking educators to do something that is not their job, and for which they are not adequately paid, and there is no guarantee that they can succeed.

It is unfair to ask educators to save the inner city black male, but the alternative is of such dire contemplation that we have no choice. **The inner cities in this** country already resemble war zones whose inhabitants are like refugees uprooted by war. These places breed crime, ignorance and degradation of all sorts. Our cities have become like enemy territory that decent people will not venture into after dark, and many of those who dwell there live under house arrest, behind bars and chains. Instead of getting better the situation grows worse. The last influence or contact the outside society has with this inner city situation is the school and the police. We will either save them with learning or contain them with bars. It is cheaper and more humane, and more American, to save them with learning. It is more tempting to contain them with bars. But, in the long run, that would make us all a little less civilized. This is the task we put before the schools. This is the burden we put upon our teachers. And as unfair as it is to ask this of schools, we have no choice but to ask. For the sake of these kids and the nation we must ask this. These young males deserve to have us give our best effort at saving them, and the country deserves to get its full measure of citizenship from them. But, even after our best effort, we may lose, and the inner city black male, who is already endangered, may become extinct, as the strong Indian brave is now extinct. But if we succeed, we will have saved for the country a precious piece of its past, a vital part of its future, and a wholesome chunk of its conscience.

"An investment in knowledge pays the best interest."
Benjamin Franklin

The Parent's Role In Quality Education

Most of the reforms and suggested reforms in education today are centered around the school. Communities are calling for better teachers, better facilities and more state of the art equipment. In this clamor to improve the quality of education, one very important component of schools and education is being overlooked, the role the parent can and should play in the child's education.

The preponderance of research in the area of parental influence on child development shows that the single most determining factor in the outcome of a child's life is the education of his mother. This influence should not be ignored when one considers education. If parents want their children to have a quality education, they can no longer demand that the school accomplish this alone. Parents must join the school and participate in their children's education.

<u>Generally, those students who are the most successful in school come from homes where parents are involved in their education</u>. Teachers and administrators should start encouraging more vigorously parents to make positive contributions to the education of their children, not just in grade school, but in high school also. One of the reasons for the failure of desegregation has been the refusal of black parents to work along with the schools and the new communities to help their children achieve the maximum educational benefits. To go a step further, one of the failures of inner city schools has been, and continues to be, a lack of involvement by parents of students in those schools in the educational lives of their children. Education is hard work, and its pursuit is often tedious and boring. It is unrealistic to expect a young child to diligently pursue education alone. Most children need the help and encouragement of parents.

Parents may feel that if they don't have a college education themselves, they are ill-equipped to help their children in school. Supporting the child and the school does not have to be dependent upon the amount of formal education the parent has. <u>It is true that the more formal education a parent has, the more educationally enriching the interaction can be between parent and child, and currently, the parents with the most education are most involved in the education</u>

of their children. But quality parental involvement does not have to be dependent upon the amount of education the parent has. In years past, particularly among black parents, many of them had very little formal education, but they inspired their children to high educational achievements. There are many positive things the parents can do regardless of the amount of formal education they have.

The first thing parents can do to help their children in school is to set educational expectations for them and demand a serious effort toward meeting those expectations. Expectations go a long way with students. In spite of the fascination with doing their own thing, children usually seriously attempt to live up to the expectations set for them by their parents. Parents who expect their children to succeed in school and express those expectations in positive ways are a great help to their children and the school. **If parents expect excellence, they are more likely to demand it and help provide those things that will lead to it**. Parents should provide children with wholesome educational materials and an atmosphere conducive to academic growth. Parents should make sure their young children have wholesome reading materials from the time they first start reading. **Good reading habits like good eating habits can be fostered in a child by its parents**. If a parent instills good reading habits in a child, the child will not quickly stray from them. Sometimes it is just a matter of parents nurturing good reading habits after a child has developed them.

In addition to fostering good reading habits, parents should realize they are their children's first and most influential teachers. No counselor or teacher will be able to totally unteach the lessons parents instill in their children, whether these lessons are good or bad. Parents should teach their children basic cooperation and respect for others, adults and their peers. **They should teach them common courtesy and what we once called good manners**. This seems so elementary, but millions of hours of teacher time are taken up every year teaching these basic lessons to students who do not learn them at home. **In fact, so much teacher time is taken up teaching things that parents should teach until there is little time left for the teachers to teach what they are educated to teach**. Parents often complain that their students can not read and do math on an acceptable level. I believe strongly that those students who do not learn what they are supposed to learn at school, are mostly those students who did not learn at home what they were supposed to learn there. It is time for teachers and administrators to tell parents: **"Send us children we can work with and we will**

return to you scholars of whom you can be proud."

Youthful readers are helped by an atmosphere that is quiet and non-distracting. Parents should make sure that their child has a private place to study and the environment is quiet enough for the child to concentrate on his studies. Parents should also maintain an active and positive contact with the school. **Too often, the parents contact the school only when the child is in trouble or has some conflict with school officials or teachers. In fact, that is probably the least productive time for the parent to go to the school**. Parents who maintain regular contact with the school will avoid most trouble their children would otherwise get into. Students should know that parents and teachers are working together and that they are never totally out of touch with each other.

The parents will, by going to the school periodically, demonstrate their interest in the child doing well. This will motivate most students. Students benefit from knowing their parents are interested in their school work. Thus, it is important that parents support their students in all of their school activities.

It is also imperative that the parents assist the school with discipline. In these days of child abuse and wild accusations of child abuse; these times of racism and unfounded accusations of racism; it is difficult to discipline other people's children without leaving oneself open to these accusations. Consequently, the disciplining of children is best done by their own parents. **The more parents are involved in school the fewer rules their children will break that require discipline**. I have lectured to parent groups at several schools. It is usually the parents of the properly behaved child who is in attendance at these meetings. The parents of the problem students are almost never there.

Few outside the school can imagine the amount of teaching time that is taken up by disciplinary problems. Even more disturbing is the fact that schools are facing these problems with students in earlier grades than in the past. **Disciplinary problems drive more good teachers away from the profession than do poor salaries**. I have met many more people who left the teaching profession or refused to go into it because of disciplinary problems than because of salaries. **Parents who send their children to school well disciplined and follow up on the child to see that the discipline is maintained, are giving that child an advantage toward a good education and a good life**. Discipline is not only good in school, it is necessary for success in just about everything else.

Parents need to sell their children on education. Many students go to school and leave their hopes at home. They don't feel that school will make a difference in their lives. This is especially true with black inner city children. It is the responsibility of parents to promote education. They should start telling their children very early how education can make a difference in every aspect of life. **Parents should keep in mind that teachers are vital to their child's education, and should, therefore, encourage positive attitudes toward teachers**. Of course, there are teachers who do not represent the profession well, but they are in the minority. The great majority of our teachers are caring, hard working, qualified persons, who have done more than any other group, outside of parents themselves, to develop good citizens for this great country. It would be a good practice for parents of young children to remember to say something good about school and the teachers. This is especially important for parents who send their children to schools outside of their neighborhoods. Black parents who teach or perpetuate hatred and mistrust toward whites put an educational stumbling block in front of their children. **Most teachers, white and black, love and care for children**. If they did not, they could hardly survive in classrooms today. Racial harmony and respect are needed in the classroom. **White and black parents need to be careful of the racial messages they give their children about the race of their teachers**. I stress this more for blacks than for whites because we have many more white teachers teaching black children than we have black teachers teaching white children. But it is a message that is equally valuable to all parents. **Racism is immoral and teaching it to one's children is irresponsible and socially crippling.** In the household in which I grew up, teachers were always spoken of in high regard. To this day, I love and honor my teachers as part of my extended family. I love the profession and am pained when I observe or hear about any member of the profession doing anything that would dishonor it. **Aside from my parents, teachers have had the greatest influence on my life**. I suspect this is true of many of our citizens.

One of the most discernible differences between good schools and bad ones is the roles the parents play in the school. Parents need to recognize the power they have to influence the educational outcome in the lives of their children. This power demands responsibility. It is more important now than ever before that parents prove that they want quality education for their children and the children of their communities. A quality education is available and can be had in any community where parents support their children and their schools.

VOICES

I want to hear my own, they say.
The voices of the past, they lied.
I want to hear from my own friends.
 Free me from the past and their sins.
Sing to me in contemporary melody .
From Iambic Pentameter, set me free,
Rap to me, Rock me.
Scream joyous sounds in my ear.
Let me be what I want to be.
 Let me hear what I want to hear.
No more sages, no more prophets,
No more Seers from the past.
My thoughts I lift up before me.
I will make them last.
I think, therefore I am.
I have eyes, therefore, I see.
I don't need ancient creeds to instruct and guide me.
I do my own thing and pave my own way.
I climb my own mountains and dawn my own day.
Leave me alone, they demanded.
Let me do my own thing.
I have my own poems to write.
I have my own songs to sing.
Leave me alone to listen to my contemporary crowd.
Their minds are fresh and their voices are loud.
What do I need with those voices from the past
Screaming their minds at me?
What I have will last.
From all the past I'm free.
That's what they said, and that's what they thought,
And that's what they tried to do.
But the voices of today will lose their way
When past voices don't come through.
But they listened to their voices
And made their own choices.
Nothing from the past did they save.
They found in their voices a multitude of choices,
And a path to an undistinguished grave.

"A mind is a terrible thing to waste."

The Education Of Black Children:
The unpublished Curriculum

Of all the essays I have written on education, this one has proven to be the most difficult. Its central focus has been the most elusive, and it has endured the most changes and rewrites. Now, after several subject changes, I have decided to just write and let what is inside of my head and heart flow, hoping that the language of the moment will do justice to the issue about which I am writing.

There are three major objectives I have for this writing. First, I want to paint an accurate picture of the all black schools that existed throughout the South in the days prior to desegregation. There is a side of this story that has not been told and the history of black people since reconstruction will not be complete until it is told. Secondly, I want to explore the question of whether desegregated schools are adequately addressing the educational needs of black children. And finally, I want to examine the issue of whether the black community can thrive without its schools. First, allow me to tell you something about the all black school I went to in Mississippi and about all black schools in general, particularly those in the South.

I assume that my school was typical of black schools, even though my sense of school spirit always tells me that mine was better than the rest. That was part of the spirit of the school. The English curriculum I studied at the school was similar to the one I taught from several years later at predominantly white schools, schools that had reputations of being superior schools. We studied, at that all black school, Chaucer's Canterbury Tales, Beowulf, the Old English Ballads, the plays of Shakespeare, the poetry of Longfellow, Burns, Keats, Browning, Pope, Poe, Dunbar, and many others. In fact, as I think of it, the English curriculum I studied at that all black school had a much greater variety and depth than any curriculum from which I've taught. I know soliloquies from several of Shakespeare's plays. I know to this day several poems I committed to memory in high school. And I have a diary I was required to keep after studying the diaries of two literary figures. In fact, I believe I remember more literature from my high school days at that all black high school in the early sixties than most students even learn today at our supposedly much better and much better equipped high schools.

My education did not stop with the curriculum. The teachers made my preparation for adulthood their mission. **They knew what the world would require of me as a black man, and they wanted to make sure I would have it.** Mr. Holloway, my seventh grade home room teacher, made sure my shoes were shined, my shirt was properly tucked into my pants, and that I had on a belt. He checked with my female teachers throughout the day to make sure I was polite and showed proper respect to women. **My teachers seized every opportunity they got to develop me in any way**. In the black school I went to we were a family, and the teachers were committed to preparing us, the children of that family, for adult life. **My black teachers had a curriculum, but they also had a commission, and they were guided more by their commission than they were by their curriculum**. In fact, their mission was the curriculum, a curriculum unpublished but clearly spelled out in the hearts and minds of every dedicated black teacher.

We were sometimes told that the white schools had better books and materials. In fact, I heard that our books and materials were handed down from the white schools after the white students were finished with them. I do not know whether this was true. (I helped unpack several boxes of new books and new science equipment over my years at the school.) But new or used books were not the issue. **Ours was a school of teachers. We learned from our teachers. They made the difference in our school day and our lives. Those black men and women loved us and saw us as their hope of gaining a little more status and respect in this country. They taught us self worth, self respect, and self direction. We read the Bible in school, we pledged allegiance to the flag, we prayed in school, and we defined for ourselves the proper roles for black Americans to play in this country. We did all of that in the black school, and we emerged, maybe not as skillful with the language as some of our white counterparts, but we had our dignity and self respect. We loved ourselves and our people. We had a purpose for being on this earth and we had a purpose for our education**.

And we all had a favorite teacher, someone who had made us their personal project and groomed us into proper and proud human beings. That is what Mrs. Williams, my English teacher, did for me. She taught me to be proud of myself, and to love learning with a passion. She taught me to speak well and write clearly. She read my poetry and introduced me to the poets of the ages. She made me believe I was important to the world by convincing me I was important to her, a much more important figure to me at the time than I ever dreamed I would be to anyone. She was the angel that brought sweet messages form heaven to a black child in Mississippi who was poor, and lonely, and unimportant everywhere else but home and at this school, and especially in her class.

The beautiful thing about my school was that there was a Mrs. Williams for every student. She was special, but there were many more like her. There was Mrs. Clark, my first grade teacher, who on many mornings came and got me out of bed and took me to school. There was Mrs. Chess, a woman of ageless beauty and endless charm, who made me a bus patrol and started me to protecting others rather than fighting them, a mission I have been on ever since. There were Mrs. Palmer, Mrs. Gardner, Mrs. Howard, Mrs. Noble, Mrs. Jackson, Mrs. Smith, Mr. Smith, Mr. Rouss, Mr. Govan, Mr. Carter, and countless others at every school who made the difference in our lives.

In the purest sense the black school was the black teacher. No group of human beings have done more to lift their people than black teachers have done to lift black people. Many of those teachers would've been considered unqualified by today's standards. Many of my teachers of earlier grades did not have college degrees, but they had love for their people; and they had the freedom not only to teach, but to lead. Every black school was an army of such heroic persons and they made soldiers out of us. Every army needs a general and the black schools had their generals.

Most of these schools were headed by strong, shrewd, dedicated black principals who knew the mission they and their people shared and the obstacles they faced, and they accepted the challenge of leading them. In turbulent times, these black men were at once disciplinarians to their black students and diplomats to their white superiors. They were proud leaders to their black teachers and powerless pawns to their white superintendents. But they walked the tight rope that enabled them to be all things to all the factions they had to appease while all the time moving closer to the goal of a freer and better society for black people. I was fortunate enough to know several of those principals personally. The one I knew best served until his death as a father figure and a perfect role model for me. I wish that every black child could have such a model. The black school was all that I have described and much more. **The story of the black school can not be**

adequately told on paper. **It is told and retold in the lives of all those black men and women who went to those schools poor and lowly and left proud and noble and prepared to make meaningful contributions to America, contributions that have made America a much richer country.** Those black schools had their limitations, but in spite of their limitations they made a great contribution to the black community, and the closing of those schools left a void in the black community that has not yet been filled.

Now, I move to the second issue I wanted to explore. **Are the white schools adequately preparing black children for wholesome lives and productive citizenship? Are they filling the void left by the black schools?** Over the years I have written much on the education of black children. It is an issue I have embraced with passionate concern, not because I, and they, are black, but because we are all Americans and I believe that all Americans ought to be passionately concerned about all of the children of America. **I would be just as vocal about children of any color who were not being prepared to lead wholesome fulfilling lives in our society. I speak and write on the subject of black children because my own background has uniquely qualified me to know about them in a way that few others do.** Someone must tell the story of these children in a language that is powerful and passionate, insightful and inspiring, scientific and sensitive, honest and helpful. I try to tell their story, as I am trying to tell it in this effort.

Education should address the needs of the students. Programs should be tailored to fit students' needs, whatever they are, if they are indeed needs that should be addressed by the schools. I am not opposed to integration. I don't necessarily think it is the best solution to the problem of educating minorities in this country, but I am not opposed to it. What I am opposed to is schools and educational programs that do not adequately address the needs of all of the students. **These needs could be addressed in integrated schools, but the problem with our schools is that they, for the most part, don't become integrated. What we have been calling integration in America has been black students going to predominantly white schools. That is not integration.**

An integrated school is one that has a student body and faculty that adequately represent the diverse ethnicities of the American population and has programs and a philosophy that address with equal interest and fervor the needs of all of the students. Such a school is rare among our integrated lot. Education can be like a tailored suit or a toga. It can be designed to meet the specific needs of a specific group of students, tailored to their specificities, or it can be a general garment that drops over everybody, and does not do anything specific for anybody. Too often the integrated school fits one of these extremes. It usually starts out addressing the needs of the white community. After a few years of integration and racial conflict, the school takes the safe approach and becomes so general in everything that no one is really helped there. Education is confrontation with ignorance. It is addressing issues that sometimes make people uncomfortable, even angry. Education is about making people better. The commercial is right when it says the best ideas are the ones which help people. **The best education is one that transforms people into the kind of beings they ought to become**.

White schools are not really adequately preparing black children for wholesome lives and productive citizenship and they are not doing enough to help them become better human beings. In the all black school I attended as a child, their main focus was making us better. All information was geared toward that end. The literature we studied was made applicable to us. The issues raised in the classroom were issues we were, or would be confronted with. **The issues in white America are different from the issues that are most urgent in the lives of black people**. White people debate such things as women's liberation, an issue that manifests itself differently in the black community than in the white community. White women want to be liberated from their white men. Black women, on the other hand, are trying to find a black man with a job to whom they can bind themselves. After one of my lectures to a group of teachers at one of the universities in St. Louis, a white woman asked me didn't I think that all of the things I had said about black people were also applicable to women. **My reply to her was that when white men and white women argue over money, they are usually arguing over whose name is going to go on the check.** However, when black men and black women argue over money, the argument centers around who's going to jail when the check bounces. The issues people concern themselves with are usually dictated by their economic condition.

The issues that concern struggling people are often different from those issues that occupy the time and thinking of affluent people. Black people can not afford to waste time in school arguing about constitutional niceties, we need to be pursuing economic necessities. We have no time to debate the role of religion in school. That is not an issue that concerns us. We have no problem with prayer in the schools. People with money have the luxury of sitting around arguing about such things. When your mother is on welfare and everybody in the house needs a new pair of shoes, the last thing you need is some affluent person telling you that you need to keep prayer out of the schools. These and other issues that are meaningless to poorer blacks take priority in many affluent white schools. Blacks could better spend their time discussing ways to improve their economic position and their image. **Every black child needs to be taught that he is an ambassador for his people, for he is, whether he likes it or not**. White schools are about moving up, blacks need to be about moving up and pulling each other up.

Black students need to be engaged in serious discourse about teenage pregnancy, self respect, racial pride, handling anger, racism, disappointment, unfulfilled dreams, and the inequality that still exists in the work place. Black males need to be challenged to continue the struggle engaged in by Martin Luther King Jr., Malcolm X, and their other black leaders, and to do something constructive with their lives, things that were done at all black schools, but, are not being done nearly enough at white schools. They are not being done because that is not the nature of white schools. White schools are for the white middle class. The curriculums at middle class schools are predicated upon the assumption of middle class status and values, they are not designed to lift kids into the middle class. This is not an indictment against middle class white schools. **Middle class white schools have very effectively educated middle class white children. In fact, they continue to do an effective job in educating these children**. It is when you place on teachers the burden of educating children who are drastically different from the students they are accustomed to teaching that they seem so ineffective.

It is obvious that white schools are not really doing what the black schools did for black students. The question is, can they. The answer is, no, not the way schools are structured today. What black teachers did with black children at all black schools, with the limited resources they had, is a hard act to follow. To duplicate that with any amount of resources would take a monumental effort and a very strong commitment on the part of schools, a commitment that the desegregated school does not seem to have. It would also take a much greater knowledge of the students at issue, information that is not widely available to teachers, and not easily attainable. It would take courage to confront ignorance and to address the area of the student's greatest need. And it would take many more black teachers to encourage and enlighten both black students and white teachers as they work with each other. **We must, as educators, and concerned Americans, do all that we can to educate black inner city children so they can lead wholesome and productive lives**. The desegregated schools can not do all that the black schools did for black children, but it is the responsibility of these schools to do all that they can do so as to offer to these students the best education America can afford. And America should settle for no less than the best education for all of its citizens.

Finally, I address the last issue proposed at the beginning of this essay, **can the black community be a viable community without the black school?** I remember from my early years of going to the movies that a church and a school were the first two things that the people established when they started new towns or communities. A school is an integral part of any community. It is the vehicle through which the community continues to give birth to itself. It is the transmitter of values, customs, traditions, and the lies we tell ourselves about ourselves in order to live with ourselves.

The black school was a very important part of the black community. It was where the middle class manifested itself and perpetuated itself. It was where the poor people came and received instructions from the middle class on how to become one of them. The black school was an integral part of the black community. Black culture and aspirations were crystallized there. The schools were a unifying instrument within the community. It was the place where the values of the community were taught and enforced, and in some cases, formulated. It was the place where the mission of the people was passed on to its children. The dismantling of the black school wreaked terrible havoc on the black community. It divided the black community and left only the black church as the unifying force in that community. Since many of the black clergy were not formally educated, and many of the black youth, particularly the black males, stopped going to church after the civil rights movement of the sixties, there was no institution left in the black community to hold together and give direction to the black community. Consequently, we now have a mindless, missionless group of people falling for everything because they were never taught to stand for anything. We have a community of blind people leading blind people and falling in every ditch in their path. We have a people who are without philosophers, theologians, or poets, and who are reduced to getting their inspiration and direction from entertainers and athletes. Such is the void left by the black school.

So we continue to explore the question, can the black community survive without the black school? The answer is a resounding no! Black people can survive without the black school, but not the black community. A group of people living in the same area do not a community make. **A Community must be held together by an institution that transmits community values and/or goals.** This was done in the past by the home, church and school working together. In the inner city we have seen a break down of the family as we knew it, a significant decline in the influence of the church in the lives of young people, and the loss of the black school. These three occurrences in concert have allowed the black community to become a gathering of desperate household of families that are connected mainly by their desperation and their miseries. What was a black community has now become a collection of cripples who make their living and their livelihood by providing each other with crutches. Without the home and the church, the school was the only hope of the inner city being a community. Without the schools, that hope is gone.

Now allow me to return once again to a lesson from the movies. As a child, I saw many movies about cowboys and Indians, and there were a few times when the Indians won. When they did, and it was obvious to the cowboys and settlers that their fort was going to be overrun and they were all going to be killed, they did something starkly similar to what is going on daily in black communities all over the country. When the soldiers gave up on saving their fort and concluded that they would be over run and killed at the next sunrise (the Indians did not fight at night), early in the morning, before the break of day, the soldiers would sneak the women and children out of the fort in a desperate attempt to save them, even though the fort could not be saved. When all hope for the survival of the community is gone, at least save the women and children. This was the message that I, as a child, got from those movies. **So, on those winter mornings when I look out of my window in the black community where I live and see black children leaving their houses in the cover of darkness, boarding buses while most of the community is still asleep, and going out of their community to schools in another community, signaling the death of their own community and the imminent fall of their fort, and the abandoning of hope by their people, I think of those western movies and my heart aches beyond description for my people and for my community.**

Given the state of the black family and the black church, no, the black community can not survive without its schools. **When the black school was dismantled, scattering the black middle class, the black community, as it had been known, came to an end.**

As I draw to the end of this effort, I can hear people saying to me, especially, teachers, what can we do? We can't go back to segregation. We can't go back to separate but equal. The truth is, we never left segregation, and black schools were never unequal because they were separate. To say that a black school is inherently unequal because it is black is to say that black people are inherently inferior because they are black. Black schools were unequal because the people who controlled the budgets for schools did not value black people and did not provide adequate funds for facilities in the black schools. An all black school does not necessarily have to mean an inferior school. What we need in this country are neighborhood schools, regardless of the color of the students. **Communities need their schools like they need their homes and their churches. Every time one of these institutions is weakened or taken, the community is weaker and poorer as a result.**

I have explored in the preceding pages three issues of great concern to me, and I must admit each has ended less than optimistically. **The black schools which were doing a very good job of educating black children have just about vanished from the American landscape only to find that the desegregated schools can't do for black children what the black schools did for them, and the black community cannot survive without the black schools.** These are painful conclusions that call our attention to the great problem we have in making America one country with one school system that serves equally the needs of all of our children. As a writer I do not always offer solutions to all of the problems I write about. Sometimes I feel a need to just call attention to the problems and point out when proposed solutions are not solving them. We will never search for new solutions if we are not clearly convinced we have a problem, and further convinced that what we have been doing is not properly addressing those problems. If this essay does nothing else, let it establish beyond a doubt that we do have problems in the area of educating African American children, and what we have been doing is definitely not sufficiently addressing them.

There is no limit upon you except the one you put upon yourself."

Emerson

Black Students/ White Teachers:
The Problems And The Promise

Since we have been deeply embroiled in desegregation, much has been written about the process, the need for it, and the benefits to be derived from it. But little has been written about the white teachers, except to accuse them of racism and insensitivity. <u>If desegregation is ever to have the desired results for black children, it will be partly because of the dedication of white teachers. Next to black students, white teachers are probably the most important players in this whole scenario and they came into this situation with no instructions, no valid information about the students, little encouragement, and little freedom to teach and to lead</u>. In addition, one accusation of racism from a black student can lead to countless meetings with principals and even threaten the teacher's job. **In the wake of desegregation some white teachers quit, others took early retirement, and some reluctantly continued to teach, seeing every day thereafter as a condemnation to a living hell**. But the great majority tackled the problem of teaching these newcomers in their classrooms and under adverse circumstances have done an admirable job. **There is still much to overcome and much at stake in this white teacher/black student relationship**.

When I think of white teachers and black students, contradictory images come to my mind. Several years ago on a talk show on a black radio station I heard a prominent black educator express great reservations about black children going to predominantly white schools. He even stated that white teachers shouldn't be teaching black children. **As a teacher and a black person I was shocked that a black man of such prominence would say to thousands of black children listening to him on radio that they should not be taught by white teachers. After all, it was black people who filed suit and forced desegregation upon the white school and white teachers**. Since that day I have heard many black educators, some much more prominent than the one I heard that day, say that white teachers should not be teaching black children. I wondered back then, as I wonder now, how those statements affect black children who are being taught by white teachers. And I wonder how white teachers, who are doing the very best they can under very difficult circumstances, must feel when they hear such statements. It certainly can't help the relationship between white teachers and black students to have the students told by prominent blacks that the white teachers should not be teaching black students.

The next image that comes to mind took place at a high school where I was lecturing to a group of white teachers about teaching black students. In the audience, unknown to me, was a white woman who was retiring after several years of teaching. I talked at one point in my lecture about the dedicated white teachers who had done their best to help black children succeed, only to be unappreciated and accused of being racists. When I got to the question and answer period this retiring teacher gave a tearful testimonial of her gallant effort at trying to help black children. She spoke of the rejection, the accusations of racism and the refusal of many of the black students to cooperate with her. The teacher did not say it, but I got the impression that her retirement was hastened by her feeling of helplessness developed from working with black children. By the time she finished, practically every person in the room was in tears, tears that I concluded, were partly a tribute or testimony to the woman's dedicated teaching career and partly a sign of their own frustration in teaching black inner city students. It is not easy teaching such students, not even for black teachers.

Students learn best when they are well disciplined, interested in learning, and fond of their teachers. Many inner city students come to the classroom undisciplined, uninterested in learning and hostile toward education and teachers. They present a formidable challenge, even to black teachers. To white teachers this challenge often seems insurmountable. But the fact is, with the great shortage of black teachers in this country, more and more black students are going to be taught by white teachers. And they don't need black men like the one I heard on the radio telling them this is an undesirable thing. Many white teachers, like the ones I just mentioned, work very hard under very difficult circumstances, to help black children, and they don't need anyone telling these students anything that will make their jobs even harder. What they need is more information about the students and more support from the black community. **The union of white teachers and black students is indeed plagued with problems, but it has promise**. The problems of this relationship are rooted in the histories, or history of the two groups, a history that has left them both scarred, and now, together they try to heal the wounds of the past. It is an effort that puts both parties through changes, but each can emerge a better being because of the experience.

Many white teachers bring to this historically troubled relationship, guilt, fear, anxiety, uncertainty, prejudice, and ignorance concerning the black child and what they and the white teacher should expect from each other. The black child often brings to this union hostility, apprehension, insecurity, racism, an inferiority complex, and a great unconfessed desire to be accepted by white teachers, if not white people in general.

These are obstacles that need to be overcome by both parties if they are to move forward in this relationship to reach the desired degree of comfort and cooperation. This comfort and cooperation will not come over night, and should not be expected to come in one giant leap. Instead, they evolve slowly and painfully through stages.

There are four basic stages black students go through with white teachers and each stage is marked by discernible characteristics. Each stage is a necessary prelude to the next, and taken together, they can be a major stride forward for both parties. **The first stage is rejection**. In this stage the black child basically denies the white teacher intimate access to his person. **The second stage is acceptance**. During this stage the child lets his guards down and permits the teacher to come in and be friends. **The third stage is a stage of decision, which leads to a second rejection by some, a dividing of the ways by some, and an entry into a fourth stage by others. This fourth and final stage is healthy, cooperative existence**.

Seldom will a black child go through all of these stages with one white teacher, and no two black students handle either stage exactly the same. These stages are much more pronounced among blacks who come from previously all black settings and come to the white teacher after elementary school. They are even more pronounced in black students who attend predominantly white colleges after attending predominantly black high schools. Each one of these stages is traumatic for the student, and some are traumatic for the teacher, but there are things the white teacher can do in each stage to make it less traumatic for both. **If white teachers understand the obstacles, the emotions, and frustrations the students are experiencing in each stage, they can help make that passage a smoother and more productive one for both student and teacher**. The white teacher can also help keep black students in school. Many black students give up along the way, particularly during the first and third stages. More information will enable the teacher to bring to these stages more understanding, hopefully with more positive results for the black student.

The first stage of rejection is easy to understand. No one wants to be rejected and we all come with our own defense mechanism against rejection. We fight rejection with rejection. **Black students reject white teachers because they think they have been and will be rejected by them**. Loving someone who doesn't love you in return is a weak and demeaning condition among people of the same race, it is more disheartening when it takes place across racial lines. These kids believe they are unwanted at white schools. **They often believe that whites don't want to teach them and that whites think Blacks are inferior beings**. This situation is worsened by the fact that the students themselves often think they are inferior and they see evidence of being put down by white teachers even where there is no such intention. In addition to what they see in school, black students get many negative message from RAP music and movies about white people that help strengthen their resolve that whites don't want them around. So to protect themselves from the emotional hurt of rejection, they reject. It is understandable, considering their history, that they would feel this way. It is also understandable when one considers that it took a court order to bring them face to face with the white teacher.

During the stage of rejection it is helpful if the white teacher is concerned, caring and honest. **The teacher should show understanding for the child's feelings, but assure him that he is there because he is an American and as an American he has a right to a quality education**. And if in the exercise of that right he finds himself in the classroom with a white teacher, then, so be it. The white teacher should not be afraid to discuss past and present injustices with black students. **But the teacher should not, because he or she is white, try to take the blame for all of the past and present injustices of white Americans.**

Out of feelings of personal guilt, some whites are willing to take on the guilt of the whole race. The white teacher should not allow black students to cast him in that guilt role either, and he should not allow them to dwell too much on the injustices of the past. The past is over and it should always be the goal of the teacher to patiently move the student forward to the acceptance of an America that is just and fair to

every one of its citizens. The teacher should challenge the student to perform so as to challenge the power structure to make available to him all of the opportunities for which he qualifies. Blacks will never know whether racism has abated if they don't prepare themselves to test new laws and take advantage of new opportunities. White teachers need to constantly challenge black students to break down old barriers, and they can not let their feelings of personal guilt stop them from insisting that black children take some personal responsibility for their progress.

White teachers should insist to black children that white people are just like all other people. The histories of all races consist of shameful deeds, and these deeds are no less shameful when they are done by whites. The white teacher might further bring to the attention of blacks who think that all whites are evil and all blacks are good, that there are taking place in Africa right now, shameful atrocities that compare in brutality to anything whites ever did. When blacks, with the truth, are brought down from their 'holier than thou' moral stance, they can better face the truth about themselves and the other races of the world. Teachers should lead them to the truth.

This is also the time that the white teacher can address the racism of black students. **Black students can be very racist**. Some Blacks feel that because they have been victims of racism, they are free to be racists. And their racism has been ignored because whites have seen themselves as the chief perpetuators of racism; therefore, they feel guilty attacking the racism of others, especially blacks. Furthermore, since blacks have been basically kept out of the mainstream and their movement and influence have been mainly in the black community where these racist views are expressed and accepted, they have not been held accountable for these views, just as the black educator I mentioned earlier was not being held accountable. It would be unthinkable for a white teacher to say on radio that he wouldn't want black teachers teaching white children.

Black children who are being educated for roles outside of the black community need to have racial views that are compatible with the rest of the country. Our country has grown in its racial outlook over the past several years. Racism is denounced by responsible persons. So, black people who wish to have views compatible with the times, must develop more wholesome racial attitudes and tolerances. The school is probably the only place most inner city blacks are going to develop such attitudes. **The white teacher, who will be seen by blacks as the chief among racists, is called upon to teach black children that racism is wrong, both morally and legally, and that responsible people**

will not harbor it, promote it, or accept it.

The white teacher should also inform his black students that they can no longer use racism as an excuse for their failures. Racism has been, and in some quarters still is, a fact of American life. But talking about it will not make it go away. **The best thing any black child can do to combat racism is to become smarter and better qualified than the racist**. White teachers should tell them that. It is an awkward position for white teachers to be put in, but that is part of the problem of this whole relationship, and that is the challenge of desegregation, and even education.

While teaching black children, the white teacher should not cheapen himself and his culture by trying to be black. **The white teacher must accept the fact that being black is something that only a black person can be. However, one does not have to be black to understand injustice, rejection, racism, and all the ills from which blacks have suffered in America**. Blacks need to be reminded that other races have, and still do suffer from these social indignities. The white teacher can assure black students that he understands those things and sympathizes with their feelings, and will try to work through all of those negatives to achieve a good education and a good relationship. This will help the child respect and trust the teacher. If the teacher is fair and helpful the trust will come in time. It will come quicker with some than with others, depending on the teacher, the child, and how they handle themselves during this stage. Patience and sincerity are virtues here. And even with patience and sincerity this can be a trying time for the teacher, and it's not an easy time for the student. The teacher can take comfort in the knowledge that this stage will pass. **Little by little, the patient, caring, persistent white teacher wears down the resistance and gains the trust of the black child**. The amount of time lost during this period of rejection is tragic for the student. The student often fails courses and falls behind his peers. Because many of these students come to the school setting with weak skills, they are impaired forever by this stage of rejection. The longer the rejection lasts, the greater the impairment. It would be very helpful for black students if this stage were shortened and they could move more quickly to the second stage. Anything the white teacher does to shorten this stage of rejection does immeasurable good for the student. For it is during the second stage, which is the stage of acceptance that the white teacher/black student relationship reaches its zenith in academic and social accomplishments.

The stage of acceptance is a very productive stage. Much can be, and usually is, accomplished in it. Sadly, however, much of the

accomplishments of this stage calls attention to the historical demoralization the black race has faced in America and the psychological impairment the black American still suffers from. All of their lives they have been conditioned that black is inferior and white is superior, particularly in matters of intellect. This conditioning has been part of their upbringing. Most of what they have seen, heard or read have confirmed this notion. The mere presence of black children in white schools is a further confirmation of that belief. Why else would their parents expend such energy to get them there? They are there to have white teachers. In the minds of most Americans, both black and white, school is a place where students go to meet teachers. All the other things that happen there are purely coincidental.

Blacks think that the reasons the schools in their neighborhoods are poor schools is because their teachers, most of whom are black, are unqualified and in other ways inferior to white teachers. They try to escape these teachers by sending their kids to white schools where they will have white teachers, teachers that the blacks naively think are going to solve their educational problems. In a sad way the presence of black children in desegregated schools confirms in their own minds the notion of black intellectual inferiority, a notion that they will have to come to grips with later in that relationship. Blacks will deny this vehemently, and I understand their denial. Who would admit that their self image is so low that they will denounce their own people in favor of the people they claim put them in the condition from which they are now trying to be liberated? However, it would be good for blacks to come to grips with their deep seated belief that whites are superior. While they languish in such beliefs they fail to accept the fact that they will have to work just as hard at a white school to become well educated as they would have to work at a black school. Being in class with white teachers, next to white students is not going to do it. White teachers can help blacks by reminding them of their own capabilities and their responsibility to live up to those capabilities.

In this second stage of the relationship the black student has a chance to experience all that he thinks he has been missing as a result of being segregated. He has now arrived. He accepts his white teacher and the teacher accepts him. He has a chance to prove to his white teacher that he is worthy of her effort and interest. He is like a kindergarten kid all over again trying to please the teacher. He sheds a lot of his rough exterior in favor of becoming a more pleasant being. **The teacher is also happy. She has broken through the wall of rejection and can now teach without confronting hostility. She feels like a missionary saving the unfortunate black child from ignorance and poverty.** This period is also salve for the white teacher's guilt. While this period lasts much progress is made, socially and academically. The child's grades improve. He accepts more of the teacher's ideas and ways and becomes more refined. He even does some things for his white teacher that he would not do for his black mama. This continues for a while, and as long as it does progress is made. **The length of this period is determined by the child, the teacher, and the experiences he has at the institution.** Black students in this stage are usually happy with their teachers and school. They attempt to integrate with the white students and become much more a part of the institution.

If the black student/white teacher relationship stayed in this stage, desegregation would be easier and more valuable. But this stage, like the first one, is only temporary. Resultingly, this relationship changes. **As the child develops his scholarship and confidence, his feeling of self worth is enhanced and he begins to see himself as equal to whites, and not so inferior any more.** The better the white teacher performs his job, the quicker the child will get to this point. Part of the purpose of the teacher is to educate and uplift, to inform and enhance. As this happens to the black child, he ceases being a thoughtless recipient of foreign ideas and becomes more of a critical thinking being. **As the white teacher helps this black child elevate his opinion of himself, he naturally ceases to hold the white teacher in such a high degree of superiority.** In time the black child even learns enough about the way whites do things to become a critic and to make comparisons. The magic wears off and he sees that different is only different, not necessarily better. **He is also a little embarrassed that he has given up so much to gain white approval.**

Unfortunately, black students do not understand the purpose of desegregation. That is understandable since no one else seems to understand it either, especially the courts and the government. **Great harm is done to black children if they are not given an intelligent rationale for desegregation, and are not engaged in ongoing discussions about it.** In spite of the caring concern they have and show for black children, white teachers still avoid discussions with them about why they are at these predominantly white schools and what approaches they are to take to this whole venture. **They do not discuss cultural diversity and how one can appreciate and learn from another culture, while maintaining allegiance to his own**. It would be very helpful to black students if their white teachers would engage them in such discussions. It would significantly lessen their trauma. But not enough of such discussions are held, partly because of the white teacher's guilt, and partly because of the black child's hostility, a hostility that surfaces quickly whenever discussions turn to race. Consequently, black children are left to come to their own conclusions about desegregation.

Many black children conclude that the purpose of desegregation is to merge black culture into white culture, requiring them to lose their black identity in favor of a white reality. Many black children at this point begin to feel deluded or tricked. They feel this is too great a price to pay for white acceptance, particularly since it often means alienation from the black community. Because they are not around many people who have had this experience, these blacks have no one to talk to about what they are going through. **This is another advantage of having a significant number of black teachers at predominantly white schools; to help black students maintain a proper focus**. It is extremely helpful if the white teacher knows what the black students are feeling and tries to help them work through those feelings. Since these students have no one to talk to, their erroneous conclusions about why they are attending white schools lead them to the third stage of the relationship, the stage of decision.

After accepting the wrong reason for desegregation, many black children react to those reasons by retreating. They conclude that they are incomplete apart from their people. They can never really be white and they think at this point that to be wholly accepted by whites they must give up their blackness. So, on the verge of acceptance, they are like shoppers pondering the purchase of an expensive item, taking one last, longing look at the price tag before making the purchase. **The black student takes one last look at what he thinks it is going to cost him to gain real acceptance by the white community. Many at this point decide not to buy, or not to buy in.**

A visit to any white college campus with a sizable number of blacks will bring you in touch with many black students in this stage of decision. Often they languish for a time wondering which way to go. Eventually, some transfer to all black schools, but most of them simply return to their neighborhoods to menial jobs or no jobs at all. And each has a story to

tell, a story of how the white society exploited him, a story that is repeated a thousand times a year to anyone who will listen. And there are always those who will listen, if for no other reason than to soothe their own sorrows and placate their own fears as they find consolation in the isolation of their deprivation. There is presently a large and growing number of blacks who have experienced this third stage of the white teacher/black student relationship. **They constitute a formidable army of disenchanted, angry people**. This is a confusing time for these blacks. They decide to go back to the stage of rejection where they do not have to deal with the constant challenge of fitting in and competing on a higher level. They choose the comfort of color and all the protection it gives them from the standards of the larger society. Unfortunately for many blacks, once they return to this second rejection they never leave. It is a rejection much worse than the first rejection. The first rejection was based upon false information. This one is based upon what he has actually experienced. He has made his investigation of white society and has found it wanting. All of the negatives he heard about in the black community concerning white people he now concludes are true. He is now more firmly fixed in his racial opinion than ever before, and what was once mistrust of whites has now become hatred. At this stage many blacks leave white schools feeling angry and cheated. They are likely to come to the conclusion that this has all been a game, that there is nothing honorable or noble about the way whites do things. It is not superior or smoother. It works for them only because they have the upper hand, a hand that will never be extended to anyone outside of the white race. This happens in high school as well as college. **Many black students go to predominantly white high schools for a time only to return to their all black schools, usually during the stage of rejection or decision, with very negative views about their experience at the white schools.**

There are other blacks who handle this stage differently. They are the blacks who decide that they will buy in to the perceived demands of giving up their cultural distinction and becoming brown versions of white Americans. These blacks put as much distance as they can between them and anything that is black. They aspire for the jobs their education is preparing them for, they tie into the value system and move through the educational system making the right contacts and connections and eventually landing the jobs they wanted. These blacks eventually bury themselves in some white suburb, never to be heard from again. They are successful, but they pay a great price for their success, a price greater than any one ought to be required to pay.

They deny their own humanity, thereby dying a cultural death, being reborn only with someone else's permission and according to someone else's definition.

The black community also pays a great price for the success of these blacks who spend most of their time and energy trying to verify their new identity and have no time or desire to make any meaningful contribution to the black community. They are usually too far away to even serve as role models for black youth in the black community. **One of the great tragedies to black individuals and the black community is that many of the blacks who leave these communities to go to predominantly white schools receive an education that has no connection to their community**. They grow up feeling no responsibility for their people and no charge to change what has fast become a disgrace to black people and America, the black community. Small wonder then that after three decades of Brown v. Board of Education the great majority of blacks who have made any meaningful contribution to other blacks and to this country were educated at all black schools. White teachers who work with black students must work to reverse those figures.

It would have been best for the people who end their relationships in the third stage to never have come in contact with a white teacher, or white school. A lot of racists emerge from this stage and they do more harm than good as a result of their contact outside of their sheltered communities. They would've helped themselves and society if they had stayed around for the fourth stage of the white teacher-black student relationship. This, I feel, is the ultimate value of desegregation. And this is where every white teacher should try to take every black child. He can do that better if he is aware of the pitfalls along the way and guide the black child through and around them. Presently too many black students are being lost along the way. They are being lost in the first and third stages of this white teacher/black student relationship. There are things the white teacher could do to avoid some of this loss. **If the black community and black educators spent less time criticizing white teachers and more time assisting and encouraging them, these white teachers could do an even better job teaching black children**.

The ultimate goal of racial understanding should not be just to know other people, but to value them. I don't know at what point we concluded that the way to achieve racial harmony in this country was to put everybody together and have them get to know each other. That was an erroneous conclusion. It cheapens people. No race should be required to be guinea pigs for another race.

People should not have to be put in cages so that others can study them to conclude they are human beings. People deserve to be accorded the human dignity common to humankind, regardless of their color. Interestingly enough, racial understanding can best be taught in one's own home without having to come in contact with other races. I was taught that I was a child of the creator, and that that creator had other creatures who were important to him, as I am important to him. Some of these creatures were different from me in color, culture and even the way they perceived the creator, but they all deserved respect. This is what people are expected to learn in the desegregated schools.   This is what they are expected to learn from working with each other. And they eventually learn it through this painful process.

Whites and blacks who endure the turbulence and stay through the problems and changes of their relationship, come to see each other as valuable and unique contributors to the richness of the human and American experience. They allow each other to remain different. Blacks come to understand that whites have their way and because of their numbers, their way is seen as the American way. They also come to understand the difference between that which is right because it is white and that which is right because it is right. They reject the former and embrace the latter.

Finally, the people who come to this last stage eventually learn that races are made up of individuals. They come to understand that every white person has a chance and a right to be different from other white people, just as every black person has a chance and a right to be different from every other black person. And they have a right to be given that chance by everyone with whom they come in contact. This is the point that we all should come to, all of the different races that make up this great nation. And this is the promise of desegregation.

It is a great problem getting people from their narrow racist positions in their neighborhoods to this enlightened world view of the human being. But that is what education is all about. That is what I learned in my home and had reinforced in the church and the humanities classes in college. The teacher now has the responsibility of doing the work of all three of those institutions with inner city students, the home, church, and the humanities class. This is a problem that would not be tackled outside of the United States. No other nation would venture such. But we are not an ordinary nation. We were conceived under extra-ordinary circumstances, and have survived, developed and flourished under extra-ordinary circumstances. We have stood over the centuries as a symbol of what men can do when they reach for that which is noblest in the human spirit. Now, we are challenged once again to rediscover America in hamlets of America where the citizens, mostly black Americans, have never realized the marvelous historical and political significance of that first discovery. White teachers, who represent the group that some will call the killers of the dream, are here now called upon to revive it and give birth to it all over in the life of every American child, particularly those in the inner cities who have been cut off from it. It is a great problem, a monumental problem, but it has such a great promise. Americans have always been willing to undertake great problems if the promise was worth it. And what is the promise? The promise is a nation where color and culture are not threats to unity, but incentives for it, a nation where black and white work together toward a common good, a nation wherein the slave master's children are at peace with themselves and their victims, a peace achieved through mutual suffering and healing, a nation where all persons are of equal value and all are justified in loving their country with equal fervor, a nation where we all, in unison, can say with equal meaning: **God Bless America**.

"The worst thing that can happen to a child is to be born to an ignorant mother."

W. L. Jenkins

Educating At-risk Black Females

Over the past several years the focus of much of the concern about at risk black students has understandably been on black males, and this focus should continue. **But while focusing on black males, the needs of others of our youth, particularly black females, should not be ignored.** And, unfortunately, **during the time we in the schools were focusing on black males, black females were becoming an at-risk group and are now failing at a rate comparable to the failure rate of black males.** Furthermore, since many of these at risk black females will likely become mothers, an uneducated, unproductive black female may be more detrimental to the black community and America than a black male in the same condition. This fact underscores the urgent need to address the problems of at risk black females.

<u>Generally, students are at risk when their intellectual, physical, emotional and/or socioeconomic condition render them more likely to fail in school than to succeed.</u> At risk students usually fall into one of four categories.

1. **They are intellectually incapable of performing at the academic level required for success in school.**
2. **Their physical and/or socioeconomic environment place them at such a disadvantage that they can not and should not be expected to perform at the required level.**
3. **They are enrolled in a school where the programs and instructions are so foreign to them and/or prejudiced against them that the barriers confronting them are too monumental to overcome.**
4. **They come to the school with attitudes and behaviors that place them in opposition to the classroom and its goals.**
    At-risk black females fall mainly into the last group. However, because of

desegregation, there is a significant number of them in the third group. **Black females who have problems with school often come to the school in opposition to the classroom and its goals, and those who attend predominantly white schools sometimes find a school system whose programs and instructions are so foreign to them and/or prejudiced against them that without special focus, the barriers confronting them are too monumental to overcome**. Helping black females overcome these barriers is the challenge facing those schools as they try to educate them. Teachers are being asked to take these at-risk black females and teach them how to become productive citizens.

Ironically, this request comes at a time when many of our large cities are involved in desegregation programs, and a great number of black females are in predominantly white schools. **White teachers, who make up almost exclusively the teaching staff at predominantly white schools, have great difficulty understanding and relating to at risk black females**. Their efforts are further complicated by the fact that the programs at these schools are designed for white middle class students.

This is not to suggest that at risk black females have no problems in predominantly black schools. **Black teachers, like white teachers, come mainly from the middle class and often know as little about these problems females as do whites**. However, because they are black and have a better understanding of the forces that shape the lives of black people, black teachers may be, in many cases, better able to connect with at risk black females than white teachers. **But the fact remains that at both predominantly white schools and predominantly black schools a disturbingly large number of black females are failing in school and choosing life styles that are damaging to themselves and the country**. These life styles are so prevalent in their communities that it is difficult for these females to escape them.

Consequently, **black at-risk girls arrive at the school having already been heavily influenced in their communities by attitudes, opinions and behaviors that make them more likely to fail than to succeed, and without special help most of them do indeed fail**. Identifying black at risk females early and focusing on their needs will speed up the process of reclaiming them and steering them toward productive lives. There are some distinct, recognizable traits that are common in most black at risk females students.

1. **They are arrogant and hostile.**
2. **They are loud and unrefined by the larger society's standards.**
3. **They have little desire to change because they are unaware of the rewards of such a change.**
4. **They are sexually active but not sexually sophisticated, resulting too frequently in teenage pregnancy.**
5. **They are unskilled in developing proper, positive relationships with success bound males.**

These are traits almost all at risk black females share, but I hasten to add that all black girls are not at risk; not even all black girls reared in the cities are at risk. **Being black and from the city do not necessarily mean being programmed for failure. But the fact is that this is the condition of a significant enough number of black girls so as to demand special attention, and left unattended it will cause a significant impact on the health of that community and the nation.** Teachers must be careful not to start expecting to find these traits in every black female and seeing them in black females who don't have them. There is the danger of labeling every black female as an at risk student, which would be unfortunate for the teacher and the student.

For those females who are at risk these five traits are the baggage they bring to the school, making them an enigma to the teacher and rendering them more likely to fail than to succeed. These students are unlike any others the teachers have had to work with before, therefore, what the teacher knows about students of the past is often inadequate with at risk black females. Even the curriculum that was useful in the past is often ineffective with these students. **But, with the right information and approach, at risk black females can be reached.** If school districts and teachers will employ the understanding and boldness necessary to help them, black at risk females can be guided into productive citizenship. But first they must be reprogrammed to be success bound rather than failure bound. This reprogramming must include addressing each aspect of their character that contributes to their being at risk and altering those characteristics, beginning with their great hostility and arrogance.

The black at risk female comes to the school hostile and arrogant, expecting and braced for conflict from fellow students and teachers, and when there is no conflict she creates it with both students and teachers, often resulting in suspension for fighting or insubordination. These females wear their hostility like a badge of honor and arrogantly project themselves into such conflict. Since it is impossible to teach through this hostility, these females can get on with their academic course work only after their hostility has been addressed and neutralized. **Hostility blocks out the warmth and sharing of any information the teacher has to exchange with the student**. The friendly, cooperative relationship between teacher and student needed for success in the classroom is thwarted. Success then, for these females, depends largely upon the teacher being able to disarm them of their hostility and prepare them for the instructions they will need to become successful in the larger society, thus helping them achieve the education necessary for that success.

If black females are to embrace education as a ticket to a better life, they must first be convinced that access to opportunities outside of the black community is more desirable than the bleak existence that awaits them if they are confined to those communities, and they must be further convinced that that better life can be achieved through education. Since these females come to the classroom unaware of and unconcerned about the promises of the larger society, they have little incentive to change. They know next to nothing about Corporate America and have few dreams that extend very far beyond their front doors. Therefore, they could not care less what people out there in that world think of them, teachers included. In fact, they have no idea how different they are from those people. **Black females come to the schools quite content with the roles assigned to them in the black community and are not impressed with the opinions of those who do not represent that community**. One of the sad facts of inner city life is that the victims of that existence do not know how out of step they are with the rest of the world. Consequently, they have no desire to cultivate the social graces that are approved by the larger society because they do not know how that cultivation would lead to acceptance and success in circles that have much more to offer them than their communities.

Teachers can help at risk black females see that education is also about refinement. Ideally, one does not just get an education, one becomes an educated person. In successful society how one acts is one of the barometers used by many to determine one's intelligence. Teachers can help these students see that if they don't act the part of intelligent, refined women, they will never be accepted as such, and will never reap the social and economic benefits of a formal education.

Teachers can help make this point by exposing these females to educated, refined black women who exemplify what they could become. It would be good and convenient if such role models were on the staff at the school. But if they are not, and even if some are, other such women should be brought in from outside the school to demonstrate to these females what is possible for educated and refined women.

Teachers, with the help of these other role models, can help these young ladies see that these are promising times for women. The opportunities that have developed in the last twenty years are staggering. Black women have not yet taken advantage of all of the opportunities available to them. **Teachers can inform these females of those opportunities and prepare them for worlds beyond their wildest dreams**. If black at risk females could ever see the great benefits of an education they would be more willing to give up some of their ways and embrace the behaviors that will lead to the rewards they seek. They would trade their loudness for sophistication and refinement.

It is an unfortunate fact that what makes the black female quite normal in her own neighborhood often alienates her from many people outside of her neighborhood. Black at risk females need friendly professionals who will bond with them to groom them for successful lives. In these times when life is more challenging, the times more demanding, and the rewards more plentiful, this need for bonding and guidance is greater than ever, and it is ironic that these students who need friends so desperately are so difficult to befriend. **Teachers who can survive their initial rebuff and be there when the students invite them into their confidence can work wonders with them**. These teachers will sometimes find some very rewarding and enduring relationships. They will frequently discover behind the loud, unrefined black exterior, a quiet, lonely, promising black sophisticated woman waiting to be born and the right person at the right time can help with that birth.

Unfortunately, at risk black females don't have just one thing wrong with them, they have many. To address one without addressing the others would leave them still crippled and unable to keep up in a competitive society. One of the most crippling characteristics of at risk black females is their sexual attitude and behavior; so, those who would help them must also address that attitude and behavior. At risk black females are often made even more at risk by unwanted or unwise pregnancies. Many of the young ladies I have worked with had at least one child when they entered tenth grade, and some had more than one. Since these pregnancies defeat the efforts of the school, if schools don't address and change the sexual attitudes and practices of these students, the school's efforts at educating them will be wasted. Therefore, schools would do well to address the sexuality of these females, teaching them that they are more than baby machines and that there is more in life for them than mothering.

Teenage pregnancy is a burdensome problem in the black community, contributing greatly to the cycle of poverty and ignorance among the black poor. When poor females have children before they are able to provide worthwhile lives for them, they insure continued poverty for themselves and almost certain poverty for their children. In essence, the black poor, with unwise and irresponsible sex, continually reproduce losers who commit much of our crime, make our streets and homes unsafe, overcrowd our prisons, increase our homicides, and lower the quality of life for all of us. **At best, the children of these at risk black females become the dishwashers and errand people of our society, always lingering at the bottom of the economic ladder because they are not equipped to compete with their better prepared citizens who are born to families more able to properly rear and educate them**. Black at risk females come out of an environment that accepts this grim reality as normal and as long as they do they will continue to practice that behavior. These young ladies must be taught that a black baby deserves more than a teenage mother can give it. Furthermore, they must be told how selfish it is to bring children into the world and condemn them to such a fate. They must be taught that their action says how little they value the life of a black person. They need to confront the bold truth that teenage pregnancy is not cool; it is selfish, irresponsible, stupid, and in a technical sense, child abuse. Teachers of at risk black females are asked to help get this message across to them.

Changing the sexual attitudes of the black poor will not be easy since they generally believe that child rearing is the natural thing for women to do. **Because of their religious beliefs, black people have never, in large numbers, embraced abortion, and because of welfare some have been encouraged to have babies without facing the fact that rearing children is an expensive, time consuming, and sacrificing endeavor that should be taken on only by those who are financially and emotionally up to the task**. Black girls should be made aware that this country can no longer afford to have its poorest citizens continue to compound its social problems through their sexual irresponsibility. They should be warned that if they do not exercise more responsibility in their sexuality, the government will likely soon impose controls upon them. This should be stressed as teachers confront at risk black females about teenage pregnancy.

Another way teachers can address teenage pregnancy among black at risk females is by addressing the social void that many of them hope to fill through their pregnancy. Many at-risk black females have low opinions of themselves from living in a world of limitations and loneliness with no one to claim as their own. They get pregnant with the notion that at least they will have the child. They even think that getting a child will bond them closer to the father of the child. But, in too many cases, the father is driven rather than drawn by the pregnancy, and the child, too often, is a demanding creature that proves too much for the child who is its mother, and consequently, lands in the household of its grandmother. This is a fact that teachers should continue to bring to the attention of black females.

Teachers can further combat teenage pregnancy among at-risk black females by raising their awareness and expectations. Too often these females who have been shut off from the great progress made by women since the sixties, have terribly limiting ideas about what they can become. They think the height of their possibilities is having babies and going on welfare. Teachers can show them that there is much more, and that even if they plan only to rear children, they need a good education. Their children deserve at least that much. They need to know that there is no job more demanding and more important than the rearing of children. That should be obvious from the trouble America is having right now managing the children of the poor and ignorant. It is a fact that a great percentage of these problem children are black, with parents much like the at risk females we have in our schools today. Addressing the sexuality of at risk black females is a must for schools that are serious about helping them.

Closely linked to the problem of teenage pregnancy among at risk black females is their inability to choose male partners who are positive and productive. These students often shun well-mannered, intelligent, success bound young men in favor of males who are more rugged, less conforming, less well mannered, less ethical in their behavior, and less intellectually inclined. In fact, many of these females insist that their boy friends have such behavior and they discourage them from practicing behavior that will lead to acceptance and success later in life. By so doing the black female helps produce the shortage of black men about which so many black women complain.

Teaching black at risk females how to choose good partners would provide them with a valuable skill. **Black girls growing up in inner city neighborhoods see very few young success bound black males who are respected for having middle class values, but they are bombarded with males who have life styles that too often lead to death, prison or a life of unemployment. Since this life is embraced and glamorized by so many of the young males in these communities, black girls come to see these traits as desirable. Such females have their sense of manhood vastly distorted, and as a result, choose males who will be forever boys. Black at risk females need to be taught to appreciate males who have qualities that will lead to enduring success.** For most black males, there is no future in playing sports, selling drugs, talking jive, being hipped or cool, or being laid back, therefore, females who choose such males are tightening the bolts that tie them to the economic basement.

Success bound females usually are attracted to success bound males. They want men who are articulate, men who can and do read, men who spend more time in the library than on the basketball court, men who belong to a family rather than a gang, and men who are headed for an office rather than a cell. At risk females too often choose the losers; some because they can not discern between the losers and the winners, and others because they think the losers are all that they deserve. Teachers can help black at risk females see that they deserve success bound males, and teacher can help them recognize the attributes of enduring success and teach them how to choose young men who have those attributes.

The teachers of at risk black females must help them choose men who are not only compatible with what they are, but also with who they are becoming. Hopefully, they are becoming successful, proud and dignified women who will be able to cope effectively with the demands of the twenty-first century. They will need men who will be compatible with such women. Teachers can help them develop the skills to recognize and choose such men. By so doing, teachers will rid the at risk black female of one more fault that places her at risk, and thereby, make her more likely to succeed than to fail.

That is what at risk is all about, being more likely to fail than to succeed. **Black at risk females come to the school so out of step with the program that they are more likely to fail than to succeed.** We can continue with business as usual and let them fail, or we can institute programs and execute approaches to help them succeed. If we choose the latter, information about the characteristics that place them at risk will help us understand them and design programs around their needs.

When the schools tackle and begin to make progress on these character problems they can then attack the academic deficiencies of at risk black females, focusing on scholarship and demanding from them the excellence that society demands. When they get beyond the rough exterior of these females, teachers will discover some very good minds. The quicker we arrive at the point that the students can focus on the curriculum, the quicker we can prepare these females for the life that is available to them, and the quicker they are prepared, the sooner they will have the rewarding life that they deserve. Many of these black at risk females come from homes and communities where they meet no one who can give them the proper directions to get to where they could go. School is the only place they can find such direction. **Teachers are the only ones who stand between black at risk females and total disaster. So, we turn to schools and teachers once again to save what would be lost without them.**

I know the task is a difficult one. To some, it may even seem impossible. Indeed, it may well be. But before we write it off as such, allow me to tell you about a teacher I know who taught at the high school I attended as a child. I was never in this teacher's class. She taught Home Economics, and at my school at that time, boys did not take Home Economics. However, I visited her home frequently, and still do. Her son was, and still is, a close friend of mine. We are all like family.

This teacher's name is Mrs. Palmer, or, **"Old Mrs. Palmer,"** as the girls at the school called her. They painted a picture of her as an old mean grandmotherly type. But in fact, Mrs. Palmer was, and is to this day, a very beautiful woman. In addition to her physical beauty, there is a spiritual beauty about her that glows and grows with the passing of time.

Mrs. Palmer took these black girls out of the cotton fields of Mississippi, out of homes where parents often could not read, and refined these girls and developed them into proper ladies. She taught them how to talk, to sit, to walk, to sew, to cook, to iron, to take care of themselves and their families, and while doing so she taught them how to show and demand respect. She taught them how to be the kind of women a man would esteem, and how to choose the kind of man that would always deserve their esteem. She taught them things as simple as female hygiene, and as lofty as womanly dignity. She taught them pleasant things and unpleasant things, all the time preparing them for a world beyond their loftiest dreams.

My sister, when she was in Mrs. Palmer's class, came home every night and talked about, "Old Mrs. Palmer," some times with affection and some times not, but always with respect. That sister, now with a Masters degree and two daughters who are college graduates, and is herself a distinguished educator; still talks about Mrs. Palmer, but now, always with great love, affection, and appreciation. She now refers to her as Evelyn, which is Mrs. Palmer's first name. My sister, and all of the young ladies who took Home Economics under Mrs. Palmer, will tell you that Evelyn made a great difference in their lives. They were at risk. In fact, all black children at that time were at risk. But teachers like Evelyn Palmer embraced their students, identified with them, claimed them, and labored with them, and by doing so they took the risk out of at risk. I believe we can do that for at risk black females today. I believe that there is enough of the spirit of Evelyn Palmer left in the teaching core in this country to save a few more young ladies. The fact that they are black and at risk, should make us no less willing to accept the challenge. It simply means the task may be a little more difficult, but if we complete it, the rewards will be so much more satisfying.

"Though a hundred crooked paths may conduct to a temporary success, the one plain and straight path of public and private virtue can alone lead to a pure and lasting fame and the blessings of posterity."

Edward Everett

Beyond Busing

Whether it is today, tomorrow, or five years from now, busing as a way to achieve educational equity will soon come to an end. It has been a tragic failure and waste, and right thinking Americans, both black and white, will have to face the fact that it never did and never will lead to the desired goals. The leaders in education, and especially those who are concerned about the future education of black children, need to develop a rational agenda for the education of those children beyond busing.

The death of busing to achieve desegregation will be mourned by some, but many, who never believed it should have been started, will applaud that day as an opportunity and mandate to educate black children, and all children, in schools that can be designed around their needs. Bussing to achieve desegregation never made sense, and from its genesis was built on a premise that was contradictory to the American way.

Busing was based upon the belief that blacks were intellectually inferior to whites and that the only way black children could get an education equal to that of white children was to educate them in white schools. The assumption was that white teachers were more intelligent than black teachers, thus making white schools better than black schools. This was the impetus behind busing, plain and simple.

Proponents of busing deny this. They say the reason for sending black children to white schools is that white schools have better buildings and facilities. But, had that been the only reason, the courts could have taken a fraction of the money spent on busing and built better schools in black communities and equipped them with the same facilities that were available at white schools, and had money left over. But that would not have addressed the assumed inferiority of blacks. That money and equipment would have been in the hands of black people, people who the courts believed were inferior and could not manage it properly.

92

Given the assumed inferiority of blacks, the only conceivable way black children could possibly get an education equal to that of white children, according to the thinking of the court, was to place them in schools where they would be taught by white teachers, since it would be impossible to achieve this equality in all black schools. If this notion of the inferiority of black people had not existed, it would not have been automatically assumed that the black school or black group would have been deprived when they were separated? The separation of equals has never spawned such an assumption before. **Every state in America has dozens of school districts that are separated from each other, and there is seldom a suggestion that the students in one district, by the very fact of their being there, are getting an inferior education, unless those students and teachers are black. It is obvious that the quest for desegregation in this country was a reaffirmation of the belief in the inferiority of blacks, a belief that was embraced as vigorously by blacks as by whites.**

Now that we have given busing ample time to solve our educational problems and it has failed, it is time for us to move beyond busing. We must get beyond court ordered busing because it was, and is, extremely wasteful and dangerous. It was wasteful in the courts, it is wasteful and dangerous on the roads, and it is wasteful in the classrooms. The millions of dollars spent in the courts presenting the case and drawing up the plans for the implementation of busing was a gross waste, and the implementation has been more expensive than the declaration. I have observed the waste from the very beginning. I have seen cabs taking students to schools, one to a car, for as much as thirty five dollars a trip. **If the American public knew of the waste that is going on in the name of desegregation they would rethink this whole issue and demand an immediate halt to this madness.**

In addition to the waste, there is also great danger to city children. Some inner city black children are bused as far as fifty miles one way, spending as much as four hours a day on the bus. **Aside from the boredom and loss of study and sleep time, those trips expose these black children unnecessarily to danger from accidents and other incidents.** There have been several bus accidents involving students being transported to suburban schools from St. Louis city where I live. These accidents have claimed the lives of two students and resulted in injuries to several others. Nationally, the injury and death statistics of these inner city black children are probably staggering.

Furthermore, as drugs pervade our society even more, the incidence of drug abuse among school bus drivers has increased significantly. More than ever before we are placing children who ride school buses in danger when they are transported from their own neighborhoods past dozens of neighborhood schools, miles away, in the name of educational equity.

If at the end of the bus ride there was some noteworthy educational or social benefit derived from busing, the danger could be a risk balanced by the rewards. But, since none of the desired goals are achieved, there is no justifiable reason for exposing children to such danger.

We must get beyond busing because there is no intelligent rationale for it. One problem I frequently encounter when discussing busing with any official who supports it, is the absence of a concrete reason for busing. In the absence of a firm statement by the government or the courts, I would suggest that the two main goals for busing are academic and social. They are, to give black inner city children access to educational opportunities equal to those of suburban white students, and in the process these black children and white children are expected to interact with each other, thereby fostering more racial understanding and voluntary integration. Neither of these two goals is being achieved.

Black children at many desegregated schools make very few academic gains beyond those they were making in predominantly black schools. The students often bring to the schools many types of behaviors which contribute to their achieving less at predominantly white schools than they would at all black schools. And as for the interaction between white students and black students, very little such interaction takes place. Black children are often relegated to basic classes, which are mostly black, and there is very little mixing of the races in social settings outside of class. After a few years at these schools many of the black students drop out as academic failures, bitter than ever from the experience. So, after spending millions on busing, we are left with black students who are still uneducated, but now, bitter and feeling even worse about themselves because they are now told that after having had the best educational opportunities they still did not succeed. It is easy to conclude at this point that they really are intellectually inferior. We do not need another system that compounds the feeling of inferiority among black children.

Another reason why we need to get beyond court ordered busing is

because of the terrible injustice it inflicts upon some of our children. It ignores the needs of the majority of our city students. It is undesirable to have any of our students believe that their education or educational opportunity is inferior to those of other children. The fact that some are being bused to so called 'better schools' says to the children not being bused that they are not getting a quality education in their own communities, and are not important enough or lucky enough to be bused out. **All children deserve a good education and there is no justification for providing it for some in a community and not for others.**

Another terrible injustice growing out of busing is the injustice done to white city students. There are many white children in city schools, but most of the programs there and the efforts to get students out, are for black students. Opportunities for educational excellence should be provided equally to all students. We should not tolerate discrimination against any of our citizens on the basis of color. It is just as cruel and inhumane to discriminate against children because they are white as it is to discriminate against children because they are black. Busing discriminates against white city children, the white children who can least afford to be discriminated against. These are the children of the parents who were not wealthy enough, or frightened enough, or racist enough to move to the suburbs at the first sign that the blacks were coming. These are also people who have shown the greatest love for the city and their neighborhoods. They should be rewarded with an equal show of concern for them and their children.

We must get beyond busing because it drains the city schools of some of their best students and contributes to the deterioration of the black community. Schools are an integral part of communities. Their best minds meet and are developed there. Taking out the best minds robs the schools of the best ideas and reduces the community to a level of mediocrity. Black communities that were already feeling the effects of the loss of much of the influence of the black church, could ill afford to lose the black schools. Such a loss is a detriment to communities. **Since desegregation was implemented in the cities, and large numbers of students were bused out of city schools to sub-urban schools, there has been a steady decline in the quality of life in those communities.** Schools and education are to enhance the quality of life; thus, when the pursuit of something that is to enhance the quality of life, by its very nature, diminishes that life, that pursuit should be abandoned.

Consequently, we should abandon busing and get on with our educational mission beyond busing. Whether we do that today or tomorrow, we will do it. Americans can no longer afford to blindly throw unlimited amounts of money into a process that has reaped no benefits. We can no longer afford to use our children, our most vulnerable citizens, as guinea pigs or pawns in a political chess game played by politicians who know little about education, and care even less about children. We should be fed up enough to stop this madness and get on with our educational mission beyond busing.

Beyond busing, opportunities for creativity and ingenuity can be embraced by school districts and individual schools. When we stop depending on busing to solve our problems we can move on to more realistic options. Local principals could respond more directly to neighborhood needs and get more involved with other organizations in the neighborhoods that work for the community good. There will be room for new ideas, new techniques, new curriculums, and a fresh new look at education. It will be an exciting but challenging time in education. It might even be the last hope of public education, and the last chance for black communities to use the schools in a productive way to save their people and communities.

There are those who will fear these times and fight in vain to keep the times from arriving. But we are definitely going to outgrow this stupidity and move beyond busing. The only question is how ready we will be and how well we will handle our new freedoms and our new responsibilities. There is a generation of city children waiting and depending on us to develop a classroom wherein they can be prepared to master the future.

"Do the thing and you shall have the power, but they that do not the thing, have not the power."
Emerson

Exploring The Issue Of Black Intellectual inferiority

Recently I was invited to lecture to a group of educators from one of the prestigious school districts in the St. Louis area. They had a serious problem in their district and wanted me to try to help impart some insight into it. Their problem was that the black children in their school district were not succeeding at the rate of the white children. They had no acceptable explanation for this. So they wanted me to explain to them what might be the reason for the relatively low academic achievement of their black students. **Their district had made considerable efforts to make sure that all of their students had equal access to educational instruction and programs and they had hoped for equal educational outcome. However, the equal educational outcome had not followed equal educational access**. They wondered why.

They had collected sufficient data and analyzed that data fairly and thoroughly, and it all pointed to one unspeakable conclusion. **On all of the tests that measured intellectual ability the white children had performed better than the black children. The whites were in the higher level classes in a much higher percentage than the blacks. The white students were doing better in the regular classes than the black students. And Blacks were far more likely than whites to be enrolled in the remedial or basic classes. And beyond the classroom, whites were scoring higher on the standardized tests than Blacks. In spite of efforts to assure equal access, Blacks students were still not coming close to equal educational outcome.** The obvious conclusion of the data was that the white children were intellectually superior to the black children. But they could not state the obvious conclusion of their data.

Even though most of these persons were white, they were not about to publicly conclude that there were some differences in the innate intellectual capacities of white children and black children. So, they wanted me, a black man, to explain away the obvious meaning of these scores and the academic performance of black children in their district, or at the very least, state for them what they would not dare state. **They were surprised when I told them the very thing they could not express, that these black children had inferior intellectual performances because they were intellectually inferior**. My position startled them.

The fact is that many of the black children we see in the classrooms today are inferior to their white counterparts. This is a difficult statement for some Blacks to accept, but it is a truth we need to confront for the sake of our children. In this case the truth will allow us to develop strategies to realistically combat the problem of the low academic achievement of black children. We should move beyond race and look at the facts of the case. It is mandatory that we move beyond race if we want to get to the bottom of this issue. **Race is not the issue here, but as long as we allow race to control discussions of the issue, we will never get to the real truth. If we were not blinded by race and frightened and stigmatized by racism, the reason why the black children in that district are not performing at the level of the white children would be so obvious**. A quick look at the children's environment, attitudes, backgrounds, and educational outlooks would state the obvious loudly and clearly. But in a racial climate such as ours, stating the obvious is often forbidden.

But let us, for the integrity of this discussion, leave the issue of race just for a moment to make sense out of this whole issue. Picture two children of any color. If you like, make them the color you are. Color is totally irrelevant in this case; the outcome will be the same. Rear one of these children in a nice neighborhood. Give him primary care-givers who are educated, mature, economically stable and good nurturers. Have these providers feed the child properly, read to him from the earliest days of his infancy, talk to him frequently, spend abundant and quality time with him, provide him with educational games and toys, and construct for him a positive environment wherein he feels loved and wanted. In short, they give him all of the things we have learned that a child should have to grow up physically, emotionally, and intellectually healthy in our society. As you construct your picture you will see that these are most of the things middle class people routinely give to their children.

Now take the other child, who could even be the twin of this first child, and place him in an environment that is just the opposite from the environment shared by the first child. Let him be reared by a single, teenage mother who got no further in school than the tenth grade. She hardly reads herself, let alone reads to the child. She knows next to nothing about caring for a child, so this child gets the very worst care. He doesn't eat properly; he is not properly nurtured. This environment is lacking in all of the ingredients essential to the health and development of the child, the things that the other child has. And the things that great numbers of the children born to poor, black mothers don't have.

Now picture these two children in school five years later. Would not one be superior to the other?   Would not the one who was fed and nurtured better be healthier, all other things being equal? Would not this child, who was also read to and taught to read, be much more intelligent in his understanding and use of words? And since he would have been properly nurtured, would he not be much more socially stable than the one who was not?   And none of this would have anything to do with color, nor would many people be surprised at the outcome. In fact, our only surprise would be if the child who was reared with all of the disadvantages would come close to measuring up to the child who had the advantages. **<u>Common sense and all of our experiences tell us that those who are born with advantage, keep that advantage and even extend it throughout their lives.</u>** Head Start is based upon that awareness.

Years ago we knew that children born to poor, disadvantaged homes were at a disadvantage in America. Head Start was developed to give such children a badly needed boost. It was to make up for the inadequacies of their home environment. Few people quarreled with the Head Start concept. We all knew that in order to give poor people a chance to run with their better-fed and better-nurtured countrymen, something had to happen to make up for what did not happen in the homes. So we developed Head Start where paid professionals attempted to do for poor children what their usually uneducated parents could not do for them.

Now, lets look at the black children who were attending that school district that needed help explaining their data. Most of those black children were bused in to those schools from poor inner city neighborhoods. **<u>Unfortunately, many of the inner city black children, the ones the parents wanted an explanation about, are coming from homes where they are not being prepared to compete with the children from better homes</u>**. We have seen some of the extreme cases paraded on television lately. I would guess that most of the cases are probably not nearly as bad as the ones we have seen on the news, but many of them are. But practically none of them are comparable to the environments middle class children are reared in. In fact, by the time these children get to school, they are inferior.

The truth is that the black poor are rearing an inferior generation of black children and the consequences will be with us for generations to come. It is very important that black people and educators understand how this is being done. Until we understand it we may continue to try to solve problems in the classroom that can best be addressed in the bedroom. **These problems in the classroom are being caused mainly by irresponsible sex, people having children that they are not ready and able to prepare for productive citizenship in our society**, which is what I told that group of concerned citizens about the education of black children and why these children were not doing as well in school as the white children with whom they were being compared.

Now we need to address the question of why these educators needed me to tell them this, rather than coming to that conclusion themselves. Why could they not look at the academic performance and test scores and conclude that these children were inferior? It is certainly the conclusion of the data. In order to understand their need for me at this point we must now return to the discussion of race.

Throughout the history of Blacks in America there has been the label of inferiority looming over our existence. In slavery we were said to be intellectually inferior. That was the rationale used by some advocates of slavery to justify slavery. It was all right to enslave intellectually inferior beings because they were not capable of having a better life on their own. This same justification was used to justify the inhumane treatment Blacks continued to receive after slavery, and for not allowing Blacks to participate fully in the political process and move into the mainstream. **As recently as the sixties, many Southern whites were arguing that Southern blacks should not have the right to vote because they were not intelligent enough to vote responsibly.**

So, we have a history in this country that strongly suggests the intellectual inferiority of black people, and we have had, until very recently, policies that were formulated around that notion. Now that we have corrected those policies, and to some degree, dispelled those notions, the last thing these educators wanted to do was to bring them up again. **They hoped Blacks would prove they were intellectually equal to whites by equaling whites on intelligence tests and**

school performance. When Blacks did not equal whites on intelligence tests these notions of inferiority surfaced again, since they were never very deep under the surface in the first place. Not knowing how to explain the disparity between the academic performance of white children and black children apart from the conclusion of black intellectual inferiority, and to avoid the whole issue of intellectual inferiority, the people who called me in to talk to them were turning for answers other than the obvious.

To discuss and understand this issue of the intellectual parity of whites and Blacks, there is a need to understand original intellectual capacity and informational deprivation. The two are often confused. It is one thing to be born intellectually inferior, but quite another to grow up in inferior conditions and fall behind because of those conditions. **In fact, inferiority may even start before birth and still not be innate.** We now know that the food and drug intake, smoking, drinking, and the overall education and life style of the mother affect the health and intelligence of the fetus even before the child is born. So, a child could actually be born inferior and that inferiority may be environmentally imposed rather than genetically predisposed.

Throughout the history of America, Blacks have been in circumstances that deprived them of equal opportunity. Therefore, their access to most of America's information and bounty was less than that of whites. So, of course, they had an inferior outcome. But that inferior outcome should have in no way indicated an inferior people. **I do not believe that any race is superior to another race; intelligence is an individual component.** There are people in every racial group who are smarter than others in that group, and smarter than some persons from other racial groups. But it is an individual distinction, not a racial one. **In fact, if I believed in the superiority of a race, the success of Blacks in America against the odds they have faced, would suggest that they are superior rather than inferior.**

Blacks are not intellectually inferior, but informationally inferior. **This information inferiority has been confused with intellectual inferiority. That has been the case in history, and that is the case with some Blacks today**. It is a given that generally people who have the best starting position will do better in the race. That is why drivers clamor for position in the Indianapolis Five Hundred, and that is why parents try to give their children the best start they can. We know that those who have the advantage at birth will usually keep that advantage throughout their lives.

Just because people are born at a disadvantage does not mean they can not close the gap between them and the advantaged group. In America, anyone, regardless of his or her station in life, can improve immensely if the individual works persistently at it. Blacks did that in the South after the Civil War. Blacks were at a tremendous disadvantage, but they worked extremely hard and made great progress. In fact, they were closing the gap between them and whites in education, family income, and other areas that indicate community well being. It is only since the Civil Rights Movement that that trend, for a large segment of the black population, has been reversed, which is why the information about the inferiority of the black students was so important. I needed to share that information with that group because they needed to know where to direct their efforts. **They needed to know that those students were inferior, and they needed to know what caused their inferiority. Otherwise, they may have thought that the inferiority was innate and, therefore, no degree of societal effort would change it**. And even though they do not want to think of inferiority when they think of Blacks and whites, it is an unavoidable issue and they needed to have the freedom to discuss it and face some truths about it.

One of the truths they needed to face was that these Blacks they were discussing were inferior to the whites with whom they were being compared, at least in the areas they were comparing them, and their inferiority was one of condition rather than color. They had an inferior start, an inferior information base, an inferior attitude toward America and education, and many of them lived in inferior environments. **Even middle class Blacks who have many of the same advantages the white middle class has, have children who are affected by some of these factors that affect poor black children, especially in their attitudes about education and the country**.

We accept the fact that these elements lead to inferior performance; we just do not like to discuss it along with race. **If environment didn't matter, if it didn't predispose one to inferiority, it would have been senseless to spend all the money we have spent on Head Start**. And it would be senseless for people to spend so much money to live in what they call "good neighborhoods."

There is one other element to this inferiority that needs to be discussed here. **The people in power make the rules and decide what is important to**

know. Even if the minds and bodies of Blacks growing up in inner cities were not weakened by malnutrition and lack of intellectual development, they would be at a disadvantage still. It is not always that children growing up in certain areas do not know as much as the children in other areas, they sometimes just know different things. And the people in power don't place much value on what is known by those who are not in power, especially if it is not copied from them. The power structure says that knowing the lines from a classic piece of literature is more valuable than knowing the lines of the latest Rap song. The power structure says that knowing how to speak like the chief executive officer of a major corporation is more valuable than knowing how to speak like the neighborhood hustler. The power structure says that knowing the latest statistics from Wall Street is more important than knowing the latest statistics from the N.B.A. **The children from middle class households often grow up in homes where the people in power live. Therefore, they naturally know and do more of the things that the people in power advocate. Such behavior is natural for them, just as it is natural for a child to speak well if he grows up in a house with parents who are English teachers. There is a double dimension to the inferiority of these inner city black children**.

When middle class white children are compared to poor white children there is almost as much difference in the performance of middle class whites and poor whites as there is between middle class whites and poor Blacks. But there is not much discussion of the intellectual inferiority of the white race because of the performance of poor white children in schools and on standardized tests.

It is terribly important that educators understand this black intellectual inferiority and its roots. At some point, we must address it, and we can address it more effectively if we properly understand it. This is not the inferiority claimed by the slave master. This is not some God ordained inferiority imposed upon us from Biblical times. This inferiority is an understandable, explainable inferiority resulting from circumstances and choices- circumstances and choices that create a vicious cycle that is devastating the black community. But this inferiority can be addressed if it is understood for what it is.

If we understand this inferiority we will see that the plight of the black child is more in the hands of regular parents than professional educators. One of the most unfortunate elements of this intellectual inferiority of black people in America is how recent trends have confirmed it rather than erased it.

Every race has its lower element. **Every race has that group of people who do not aspire for the higher things in life, either in their life styles or goals**. The black race is no exception in this respect. The tragedy of the last three decades since the Civil Rights Movement is that because of several social forces coming together, the lower element of the black race has been able to grow at a faster pace than any other segment of the black population, and much of that growth has been in producing inferior children. These children are entering the schools inferior to the other children in the schools, children who were reared by middle class families. When these students are tested they do not compare favorably with the other children. In fact, they prove to be inferior. It could be no other way.

Now, the question is, can this inferiority be fixed, and if so, how? Whether it can be fixed or not depends on what one would consider fixing it, and whether one thinks that something is wrong in a society where great numbers of people are born destined for failure. And the second question needs to be answered first.

There is nothing really wrong with being poor or ignorant. There is nothing wrong with large segments of the population having less than others in the society. **A study of the world's population, past and present, will reveal that the conditions that we say are terrible and unacceptable have been and are being accepted as normal in other societies**. The difference in America is the standard we use when deciding how well off people are and should be. That standard is more often than not, middle class white people. We think that people are not doing as well as they should if they are not living like middle class whites are living. If the black infant mortality rate is five percent and the white infant mortality rate is one percent, we say that the infant mortality rate of Blacks is terribly high. It is simply higher than that of white people. Infant mortality rate is closely linked to the life style and choices of the one carrying the infant, and the overall health of the environment in which the infant is to be born. The infant mortality rate of any group is exactly what it should be for any people doing what that group is doing to have that level of infant mortality. There is no fixed standard except the relationship between the behaviors and the consequences that result from those behaviors. **The same behaviors will lead to the same consequences for people in the same conditions the great majority of the times**.

So, when one says we are going to fix the social situation in America, we must be clear on whether we are trying to raise everybody to the standard of white folks, or whether we will accept the life styles people choose and the status that styles provides for them. I take the position that black people do not have to have what white people have, and they will not have what white people have unless they do what white people are doing to have what they have. **It is about time we stopped comparing ourselves to white people as if they are the norm and all things must automatically move toward eventually being like them. And we must stop thinking that anything is going to make us be like others except behaving as they behave**.

Why is this so important? Poor Blacks need to see the relationship between their behavior and their condition, and that their condition is normal for their behavior. **The black poor are just where any people would be if they did what the black poor are doing, and the only way the black poor are going to change their condition is to change the behaviors that are causing that condition**. Blacks and white liberals can cry all they want to about how unfortunate or unfair it is, nothing is going to change until the poor change their behavior. A change of that behavior would be the greatest testimony to the intelligence of the people. **A person's intelligence is best measured by what he does with his own condition, not how he compares with another in a different condition**. The black poor must be challenged to take their condition as it is and use every bit of energy and ingenuity they can muster to change that condition for the better.

In the meantime, we must make it clear that the people who are testing inferior are not doing so because they are black. They are testing inferior because they are born in increasingly inferior conditions and they are developing an increasing disdain for the skills that would eliminate their inferiority. The black children who are having problems in the schools today often come from problem homes. They generally do not believe in the merits of a formal education, and, consequently, do not apply themselves in the effort to achieve that education.

If Blacks are to progress as a race, they must do so as individuals and families. **Progress can be made through discipline, responsible sex, intelligent mate choices, education, hard work, mature goals and long- term vision. Progress can be made for Blacks the same way it has been made by other races, and the same way it is being made by many Blacks today. Let's not forget that there are millions of successful Blacks in this country whose intelligence could never be questioned.** In fact, if we can find just a few blacks who are not inferior, that is proof that inferiority is not racial. And we all know many Blacks who are superior in their fields.

Perhaps those educators to whom I spoke, and others who have the notion of black intellectual inferiority, and see many of the inferior young black people today as confirmation of their notions, can look at the data with new insight. **Black people are not inferior; some black persons are.**

Those parents who are having and rearing inferior black children can look at this data and make a decision about where they want their families to go. They can decide whether they want their children to be the bus boys and dish washers of their time. If they do they can continue to have children who they can not properly rear and educate. Educators can stop holding conferences and bringing in experts to explain to them what they are doing wrong, and what they can do right to improve the situation. They will know that there will be nothing they can do. The inferiority and poverty these people will be experiencing will be a result of their own choices and it will be normal for them.

But, if the parents decide they want children who can compete with the best and the brightest in our society, then they will look at what the best and the brightest are doing to produce children who are capable of carrying on their tradition of being the best and the brightest and do those things. It is their choice and in a democracy it is undemocratic to take that choice away from them. In this country people have a right to be inferior just as they have a right to be superior. We must come to see inferiority as just as normal and necessary for a democracy as superiority. **The beauty of America has always been that each individual could choose which level he wanted to strive for, and that choice should not be limited by the color of one's skin.**

I think I will not have done justice to the frustration of those educators or to the aspirations of black people if I did not address one other element of this issue of black intellectual inferiority. These new questions arrive at a time which is most inopportune for black people. It is ironic that the question of inferiority has to be raised at a time when so many things have happened that could have brought out the best in the black race. Laws have been changed to accommodate Blacks. Attitudes have been changed. New doors of opportunities have been opened. The table of democracy has been set and the buffet is ready. All of the citizens can choose freely from the great menu of this bountiful society. The generations of Blacks who have preceded this present generation worked hard to usher in this day. **The progress of black**

people has been slow, but it has been steady up to this point.

Ironically, since the Civil Rights Movement there has been deterioration from within the black race. The principles and values that brought Blacks so close to equality in America were abandoned, and thus they began a steady slide backwards. This backwards slide is represented most notably by that group of Blacks who is testing inferior in our schools.

If there is anything about this slide that equals the frustration of whites, it must be the pain of Blacks who worked so hard to come so far to see it all lost. I can relate to this pain even more than I can relate to the frustration of those educators. I feel that pain as deeply as anyone. I worked in the Civil Rights Movement and marched in the streets. I risked my life daily and denied myself many of the pleasures of youth as I pursued the virtues of the ages, freedom and equality. I stood on the stages of the great universities of this country and explained to white people why Blacks were equal to any race of people anywhere. Now, I am called upon to explain why they are inferior. What pain! It is a pain that is deepened by every new set of statistics that verify the condition of my people, a condition that is undeniable. And the pain is also undeniable. At times it becomes almost unbearable. But I have learned to bear the pain the same way I bore the injustices of the past, with hope. That is why I explained the condition of these Black children to those educators. **It is my hope that white people will understand what has happened to black people, and black people will understand what has happened to them, and together they will improve the plight of those wretched black Americans. And then white educators can get rid of their frustration and I can get rid of my pain.**

"To expect a people to be both ignorant and free
is to expect what never was and never will be."   Thomas Jefferson

The New At-Risk

Carl and Jeff are sixteen year olds who attend a middle class predominantly white school. Carl is black and Jeff is white. They are both from good families and have been taught very good values. They both have done well in school and are looking forward to graduating from high school on schedule and attending competitive colleges. They have the grades, academic backgrounds, and the family support to be successful. Carl and Jeff are not brilliant. They are average, hard working kids who have made the best out of their school time and are looking forward to going to good colleges and being successful. They seem perfect candidates for the success they seek.

But success may not be as likely for these two young men as it seems. For Carl and Jeff are members of the newest at-risk group in America's schools. **At-risk is a term that refers to those students who, because of some deficiency, either physical, mental, social, or behavioral; are more likely to fail in school than to succeed**. They are less likely to be successful than the great majority of the students. In the past, Carl and Jeff were in that great majority who were destined for school success. But now they, and others like them, comprise a new at-risk group that is potentially larger and poses a greater problem to America than all the rest.

There are influences in our schools that are causing our most normal children, the ones for whom the schools were originally built, to be placed at-risk? At least four of these influences combined create the situation we now face. They are subtle, and taken alone, neither would spell doom for the regular student, but combined they may wreak havoc on well behaved children and well intentioned educational programs. The four factors that are putting regular students at risk are: they are being ignored in favor of historical at-risk students, they are being distracted by many of the poorly behaved at-risk students, their material is being watered down to give the at-risk students a better chance of keeping up, and they are being set up for failure when they later attend competitive schools. This combination is seriously damaging the educational outlook for regular students in our public schools. Over the years each one of these factors have eaten away at the quality of education received by regular students and they started rather innocently with the first one, which is regular children being ignored.

It is detrimental to a child to be ignored. Children need attention. They need monitoring during their years of rapid physical, social, moral, and intellectual growth. If they start growing in the wrong direction they need to be corrected quickly and set on the right path. And when they are growing in the right direction they need to be assured and encouraged. But one will not know what direction children are growing in if the children are ignored. If they are ignored they can become strangers in a short period of time. Children should not be ignored in our schools; the danger of losing them is too great. **But many of our regular, well behaved students are being ignored while the energy and resources in education are being directed toward special programs**.

Administrators and promoters of special programs deny this all the way to the bank, **but the truth of the matter is that when resources and personnel are limited, one program's gain is often another program's loss. This applies to both money and personnel**. Often teacher time is taken up working with students with special needs at the expense of giving appropriate time to the normal and legitimate needs of regular students. **Some schools are so burdened with special programs that there is little money and few persons left for students who don't have the problems that qualify students for the special programs**.

Teachers are often given classes of five or six at-risk students, causing the numbers to increase in the regular classes. Consequently, many of the students who are not in special programs receive very little of the attention they need. They are ignored. This happens routinely, even though it is denied by administrators. I was once puzzled, and at times angered by this administrative denial. But I finally concluded that administrators had no choice but to deny that regular students were being ignored in favor of at-risk students. They could not admit that this was happening without showing an effort to do something about it. After all, they are the instructional leaders. Since they could do nothing about it, the next logical thing for them to do was to deny that it was happening.

The preoccupation by teachers and administrators with at-risk

students and programs often gives regular students the impression that they don't matter. As a result, some of these students develop negative attitudes toward school, and education in general. They see the at-risk students getting most of the attention and breaking rules and never having to face the consequences of their behavior. They watch standards being constantly lowered for the at-risk student. They observe these students being given opportunities to turn work in late, or not at all. And they see the at-risk students constantly being catered to, all at the expense of the regular, well behaved child. These children must feel abandoned by their educators and the system itself. No wonder they are becoming at-risk.

It is noble and right that we help students with special needs, but there is a point at which the extra time given to students with special needs could seriously cut into the time needed by students who come to class prepared and ready to learn. Regular students see their teacher-time being shortened in favor of the at-risk students. This sometimes causes them to feel that they don't matter and they become discouraged.

Many of us know of good children who got into trouble to get the attention of their parents who were giving all of their attention to their poorly behaved children. This scenario occurs in school daily. Children who see bad behavior rewarded are often tempted to adopt that behavior to get attention, or at the very least, they resent the children who are rewarded with attention for such behavior. In the end, the morale of the well behaved student is lowered, contributing to his becoming at-risk.

In addition to being ignored, and having their resources drained, the regular students are becoming at-risk because they are surrounded by problem cases that are constantly distracting them in their efforts to learn. Recently an educational study concluded that one of the reasons students aren't learning as much in American schools as they are in schools in some other countries is that they are not spending as much time at their studies as students in those countries. Upon hearing the study, some concluded that we should lengthen the school day and even the school year, a typical reaction for people who are not personally involved in schools. But those of us who are in school know that it is not the length of the school day or the school year alone that determines how much time students and teachers spend pursuing knowledge. **Much of the classroom time is spent responding to distractions caused by undisciplined, problem students.** I have had classes with several at-risk students in them and I know first hand of the instructional time that can be lost responding to the myriad of problems caused by such students.

One of the most disappointing classes of my teaching career included three at-risk students. I remember very well the class in which these students were enrolled. They were all labeled **SPECIAL** and were receiving services that were provided by the special school district for such children. Since these children were classified as **SPECIAL**, there was a limit to what I, or the administrators could do about anything they did. In fact, I took them to an administrator and told him that the students were making instruction in that class impossible. He simply talked to them and sent them back to class the next day. Needless to say, their behavior did not change. The reason the principal did nothing was because everything had to be done according to the student's Individual Educational Program, or I.E.P. This plan often contained outlandish measures that had to be taken and strict guidelines that had to be followed by the teacher or administrator when working with these students. **Students who have an I.E.P. can almost get away with murder in school.** And these three did everything short of murder in that class.

However, it is not the three at-risk students that cause me to remember that class so vividly, even though I remember them very clearly. Their pranks and childish, disruptive behavior, make them difficult to forget. What I remember most vividly about that class, however, was that I had two very well behaved young men in the class who really wanted to learn. One was an exchange student from France and the other one was a black student. They were both intelligent, college bound students, who were very much like Carl and Jeff. They wanted to learn, and came to school daily ready to learn. **But the three at-risk students saw to it that these two well disciplined students did not learn nearly as much as they should have.**

I remember the looks on these students faces as they watched these three at-risk students do some of the stupid things they did in class. These disciplined students were the losers. They were the ones who came out of that experience with far less than they were prepared to receive. I never got a chance to teach them all that I wanted to teach them about the literature we read. I never got a chance to engage them in the growthful discussions that should have been a part of that class. I never got a chance to have them write on some of the mature subjects on which they should have written. No, I never got a chance to do many of the things with them that I should have done. I was so busy working with those three at-risk students who were simply taking advantage of the label.

It would not have been so bad had this been an isolated case. But unfortunately, it was not. In that building, at that hour, there were several other teachers having similar experiences and coping with similar frustrations. Multiply that by thousands across the country and you get a picture of the magnitude of this problem. **Distractions are causing regular students to lose millions of instructional hours and billions of bits of information that they will need later in life**.

These distractions cut down on instructional time dramatically and leave all of the children academically deprived. Many of the at-risk students are given tutoring, resource room time, or skills classes that help them make up for the loss of instructional time in the regular classes, but the well behaved child gets nothing. He is ignored. He is the eventual loser.

A natural consequence of classroom distractions is the watering down of the curriculum, another point that some educators and administrators deny. They say that the same high academic standards are upheld regardless of how many at-risk students are in the class. This probably could be possible if at-risk students were allowed to fail, but they are often not allowed to fail. Consequently, the teacher must go slowly enough for them to keep up, and must water down the material so that those who hardly pay attention can understand it. When this happens the brighter students are held back. They do not cover the amount of material they should and they do not go into the material in the depth that they should. The regular students are therefore not challenged. Since they can keep up without putting forth much effort, they stop studying. School becomes too easy for them. But all the while they are making good grades and looking forward to going to competitive colleges and doing well. They are in for a rude awakening.

<u>Of all the things that schools are doing to this new at-risk group, probably the most crushing is setting them up for failure in college. At many of the public high schools the students who go through the regular programs are not being prepared to be successful at the more competitive colleges and universities</u>.

When I first started teaching at the school where I am, the regular program was academically strong. Most of the students in the regular program back then would be top students in honors today. They were in the regular program because they were not really honor's students at the time. The honors program was very outstanding. Over the years there has been a steady decline in the regular program and a steady decline in the number of students who leave the regular program and go on to competitive colleges and do well. And there has been a steady increase in the number of students returning from colleges frustrated because they were not prepared academically to do the work. They had neither the knowledge base, nor the study habits, even though they had made good grades in high school. No one told them that these courses were watered down and they were not getting nearly the information, nor being required to do the work that would prepare them for college. So, many of them leave the competitive schools and go to junior colleges to build up their knowledge base and strengthen their study habits. They do this at their own expense and on their own valuable time, all because they had a high school curriculum that was geared toward the at-risk and did not properly prepare them for life at competitive colleges.

It should be clear to educators by now, that even though we had the best of intentions, our emphasis on at-risk students for the last several years has led to the present ignoring of regular students, allowing them to be distracted, watering down their curriculum, and setting them up for failure in college; and thus creating of them another at-risk group. The regular students are the new at-risk. Now they need intervention. It is time the schools address the plight of the new at-risk. If we are to address the plight of these students, who deserve more than any other group our sincere attention to their needs, there are some things we must do.

We must first be honest about the risk they face. Educators will not admit that their attention to the at-risk groups has significantly diminished the quality of education the regular student receives. Administrators defend their special programs and the money spent on them with the claim that it makes for a better school environment for all of the students. But that is just not the case. **Special programs for the at-risk deprive regular students of services and teacher time.** It is so obvious that it seems almost ridiculous to argue otherwise, but some administrators and teachers insist on arguing otherwise, even though it is an empty argument. Those who have any knowledge at all about the way schools are run and the amount of money available for teachers and programs know that these special programs are taking away from the regular program. Administrators need to admit that and move to the next step.

Once we face the truth about what has happened under our present system, we must move to redefine at-risk. The declaration of students as at-risk in order to address more specifically their needs in the educational setting to assure they got as much out of their school experience as possible was a beautiful idea. It was a noble, well intentioned thought. But, like many of our noble thoughts that are well intentioned, something happened between conception and implementation. **The original idea behind at-risk was that students who, through no fault of their own, had some condition beyond their control that kept them from being able to succeed in public schools without intervention or special help, would be given that intervention and/or special help in a way that would not hamper or interfere with the education of the other students**. That is a wonderful idea and probably very few Americans would oppose it. But that idea opened up the flood gates and everyone from severely handicapped children who need special electronic gear to hear and communicate with the teacher, to rowdy, obnoxious children who simply do not want to comply with the school rules, qualify as at-risk. And many from both extremes are taking advantage of their status. **Most of us are sympathetic toward children who are physically handicapped and need special assistance.** However, we recognize that the public schools are designed for children who are physically and emotionally able to handle that setting. **Students who have extreme deficiencies, whether they are physical or emotional, are not served well in our public schools. Furthermore, our attempts to serve them, when taken to the extremes, do harm to children who do not need these services. And we do not do much good for the children for whom we are taking these extreme measures.**

Having said that, students who have extreme deficiencies are generally not the children who are causing most of the problems that put the regular children at risk. **Severely handicapped children are not disturbing the educational setting. They may be requiring more teacher time, but their presence in the school is not much of a factor in the decline of the academic integrity of the school.** The problem is caused by that great number of people who are not at-risk at all, but are simply poorly behaved children who want to have their way at the school and they seek the label of at-risk to help them escape accountability. They are children whose parents will not take proper responsibility for supervising them and making sure they comply with school rules. **These children are disruptive in school because they are allowed to be. There is nothing wrong with them that would keep them from obeying the school rules. They just**

don't want to, and once they are classified as at-risk, they don't have to. So, they don't.

If we are going to save this new at-risk group, we are going to have to lower the numbers of the other at-risk groups. The system can tolerate those who are truly at-risk, for their numbers are manageable. But it can not take on scores of people who are simply running from responsibility.

Beyond redefining at-risk, the advocates for the new at-risk group must be as militant and vigilant as the advocates of the other at-risk groups, who have fared well in education because of the efforts of their parents and other special interest groups who have intimidated educators and legislators with unfounded law suits and threats and wild claims of discrimination. **And out of fear of law suits administrators bow to the pressures of such groups and give them whatever they ask for, regardless of how outlandish the request, and regardless of whether it is in the best interest of the students they claim to represent.** And many of their requests are definitely not in the best interest of students, the ones they claim to represent, nor the others they have put at-risk by their efforts.

I feel that much of the aggressive lobbying of parents of at-risk students stem from their own guilt for what they feel they may have done to put their children at-risk. Their interest often goes far beyond what is in the best interest of the child. It is obvious that many of them have reasons for their efforts that have nothing to do with what is best for the child, or what is best for education in general.

Because of the aggressiveness of the parents of these other at-risk groups, it is necessary for the parents of this new at-risk group to make their voices heard. After all, the "squeaking wheel gets the oil." This group must make it clear that they are not anti at-risk, especially the legitimate at-risk. They should affirm that they are concerned about the education of all children, **but that genuine concern for all children should not mandate that they stand by and watch the public schools become a place where their own children can not get a quality education.**

The new at-risk group needs the outrage of their parents to be evidenced in the market place. Legislators, administrators, and educators need to hear from parents of average students. **Their message needs to be unequivocally clear: "We want our public schools to be places where average children can get a good education."** when that message is heard the message that is promoted by the parents of the other at-risk groups will not be as loud and as intimidating as it has been in the past.

The teachers must also get involved by again becoming champions of the regular citizen, allies of the average. In order for the parents to know what is going on, teachers must tell them. **Few parents know what goes on in the school on a daily basis, therefore, teachers must serve as a link to the home and let the parents of regular students know what is happening to their children.**

Teachers should take a stand and say when enough is enough. Although they want to give each child as much of their time as they can, and want to address the needs of all of the children in the school, teachers need to recognize and accept their limitations. **The fact is that sensitivity training, workshops on the at-risk, nor more courses in psychology, are going to enable teachers to be all things to all students, and be effective.** Therefore, they must make intelligent decisions about how they spend their time in the classroom and they must insist that that same intelligence is employed by administrators when they plan special programs for students who are at-risk.

We must also accept that all children have special needs, and to ignore those needs is to create an urgency that turns ordinary situations into crises. We must see that when we too heavily focus on one group at the expense of another group, we often create in the latter group what we are trying to solve in the former group. That is what we are allowing to happen in education. By our over attentiveness to illegitimate at-risk groups, we have created another at-risk group that is growing daily while we ignore it. We must halt this madness and come to our senses. For if this new at-risk group is allowed to grow to its full potential and engulf the great majority of our average students, there are no programs and resources that will be sufficient to restore them to their health. And if we lose this group we may well lose the country; for it is on their shoulders that the very pillars of our Democracy rest.

Before I leave this essay, I feel I should address those who would ask the question, what does this essay have to do with black people and why is it included in a book entitled Understanding And Educating African-American Children? It might not be apparent on the surface, but this essay has quite a bit to do with black children. And even if it didn't, it is something I would be quite concerned about. I am very concerned about the state of public education, and anything that threatens to bring the quality of education down in our public schools concerns me.

But it does have a direct connection to black people. **Blacks, more than any other group in America, depend upon the public schools to educate their children and lift their race.** If those schools are burdened with problems they will be less capable of elevating anyone. Most of the successful black Americans were, and continue to be, educated in the public schools. So it is in the best interest of blacks that the public schools remain good schools.

Another way this issue of the new at-risk affects Blacks is that many of the at-risk children who are disturbing the educational environment are black, and many of those who are being denied a quality education as a result of these disturbances, are black. The class I mentioned in which the three at-risk students distracted everyone else is a typical example. The three students were black and one of the college bound students they distracted was black. That student had difficulty getting into college and wound up actually going to a Junior college because he was not prepared for the more challenging academic programs that he would have faced at a four year school. And part of the reason he was not prepared was because of classes like the one he was in with those distracting students.

Furthermore, almost all of the at-risk students are placed in the regular or remedial classes, where Blacks generally are. Whereas, exceptional white students still get a decent education in the honors programs in the public schools, Blacks represent a very small percentage of the students in those courses. So, if the regular programs are destroyed, Blacks' chance of a good education is destroyed.

Beyond that, many of these at-risk students, who are not really at-risk but are using the label to escape responsibility, are black children. Some white school administrators quickly label black children as special or at-risk, and these children are allowed to go through the school creating an environment where neither they, nor anyone else can get the education that should be available to them in public schools. This happens frequently at predominantly white schools. As long as it continues Blacks will continue to fall farther behind. **Black parents, more than anyone else, ought to be outraged by this occurrence and should be doing whatever is necessary to restore quality education to the regular programs in all of our public schools**. Blacks can ill afford to have their children survive the perils of neighborhoods that place them at-risk only to go to school and become members of a new at-risk group.

"The more the mind does, the more it can do."
William James

A Heart To Heart Talk To White Teachers Of African-American Students

Over the years I have been asked a great number of questions by white teachers about African-American students. In fact, this book grew out of questions. After every lecture several people would approach me and ask questions about the subject on which I had lectured and about other issues relating to the education of African-American children. Even now, after each of my lectures there is a question and answer period, and certain questions persist. **Regardless of the location of the event or size of the audience, white teachers always express common anxieties and frustrations about teaching black children.**

One of the limitations of reading a book is that one does not have the author there to answer questions about any of the issues raised by the reading, and this book is no exception. Some of the readers will have questions or concerns that don't merit an entire essay, and therefore, are not addressed here. And some of the issues those questions surround will not necessarily fit smoothly into the discussions that are covered in the essays in this book. So, I am including this essay to focus primarily on such questions. These questions are not necessarily related to each other in any way except that they are all from white teachers who are concerned about black children, and they will all be treated with the utmost concern and thoroughness.

I think at this point it would be appropriate to explain why I titled this effort, A Heart To Heart Talk To White Teachers. Of course, the material covered here will be good for any teacher. **I am convinced that all of us who grew up when times were different, and have been removed from the neighborhoods where this generation of African-Americans now live, could benefit from knowing more about what such children are like today.**

When teaching African-American children, **African-American teachers have an advantage over white teachers because they, being African-American, can at least relate better to the history of the African-American children, even though they may be shut off from their present experiences**. But all teachers would be helped if they had a greater understanding of today's African-American child.

There is a uniqueness about the white teacher that separates him or her from the black teacher. **White teachers have had the luxury of going into teaching simply to teach. Because of the stability of the white community and the number of professionals other than teachers, white teachers, more often than not, could focus mainly on teaching. They did not have to be the minister to the child. They did not have to be his politician or civic leader. They did not have to be his financial counselor. They did not have to help him maneuver his way through an unjust society. Their main job was to teach. There were others to give white children all the assistance they needed in the other areas of their lives. This luxury allowed white teachers to go to their classrooms, teach their subject matter, grade their papers, and concern themselves at school mainly with teaching. What a great life! It must have been nice**.

As a black teacher, I have at times needed to be much more to black children than white teachers needed to be to white children. I have needed to be their minister, their politician, their social worker, their civic leader, their representative with middle class white America, and their guide through a racist, unjust society. Consequently, I have had to think through just about every issue relating to black people. Therefore, I have opinions on these issues, not because I enjoy it or want to, but because I felt I had to if I were to be an effective teacher of black children.

White teachers, on the other hand, have not had to think of these non-education issues. They have simply had to teach. That is why some of the questions posed by white teachers sound naive and insincere to black teachers. Some Blacks even get angry at the kinds of questions white teachers ask. Black teachers think the answers should be obvious. But they are not obvious in a climate such as ours. At a time when the most innocent statement or action can have you labeled a racist, and can even jeopardize your employment, it is natural for persons of any color to exercise extreme caution as they tread into unknown territories.

There are other differences between black and white teachers that it might be good for black teachers to remember when they are tempted to get angry with white teachers about the questions those teachers ask. **Blacks have always known more about whites than whites have known about Blacks. Whites could ignore Blacks, but Blacks could not afford to ignore whites. Blacks needed whites, but whites did not need Blacks. Blacks have always**

been exposed to whites, but whites have not always been exposed to Blacks. Blacks could read about whites, but whites could not as readily read about Blacks. Blacks could hear whites on radio and see them on television, but whites could not often hear Blacks on radio or see them on television. Our whole culture was dominated by the thoughts and aspirations of white people and Blacks learned much about whites as they involved themselves in this culture. Much of that has changed, but the teachers we are talking about are not teenagers. And in their formative years these changes had not taken place. And even now, the kind of knowledge one is exposed to in the media about black people is very limited. So we still have white people who have a tremendous lack of good information about Blacks, and many of those whites who know very little about blacks are teachers. That is why I treat questions by white teachers very seriously and try to answer those questions sincerely and thoroughly, which is why this essay is included in this book.

One of the questions white teachers want to ask but are often reluctant to ask in a public forum is, **"Should I be teaching black children?"**

This may sound like a ridiculous question to some black teachers, but I can clearly understand how white teachers get mixed signals on this issue. There are those who think that white teachers should not be teaching black children and they are very vocal in expressing that opinion. Recently I lectured for the Cincinnati Public schools. After my last lecture the administrator followed me to my car and told me that I was the first African-American speaker that her white teachers had enjoyed. She said that the other African-American speakers had condemned the faculty staff and told them they had no business teaching black students.

There are African-Americans who think that white teachers should not be teaching African-American children. I feel that that is an illogical and irresponsible position. **I would be embarrassed and angered if anyone told me I could not teach white children, particularly after having the great majority of my white students over the years tell me I am their favorite teacher**. I would find this unacceptable for another reason that may be even stronger than my positive experiences teaching white children.

When I was growing up in the South I knew many white families, and almost all of those families had black women who practically reared their children. These black women prepared every meal for these white children, kept them for long periods of time while their parents were away, and taught the children almost all they were expected to learn about personal behavior. If black women can rear white children, certainly white teachers can teach black children.

So, the answer to the question, should white teachers be teaching black children, is yes, they should. In America, we can have it no other way, particularly since our society is as it is and people have their personal freedoms to live wherever they wish and make personal choices about their lives and where they will attend school.

<u>**Blacks who think that white teachers should not be teaching black children need to be reminded that it was not white people who filed the law suit and demanded the desegregation of schools**</u>. **That court action that led to the integrating of America's public schools was initiated by Blacks**. It is a contradiction to demand that black children go to predominantly white schools and then demand that only black teachers teach black children. Such a demand would nullify two of the values of desegregation, which are racial interaction and understanding.

If black children are to have only black teachers, then they should be in all black neighborhoods attending all black schools. That may even be better for them, but that is not the discussion at this point, and that is not the reality. **The reality is that they are in white schools all over the country and it is pointless and irresponsible to suggest that they should not be taught by white teachers**.

Another important point to be made here is that teachers are professionals. Professional people should be able to perform their profession with, or on anybody. It is a standard that we have challenged all professionals in this country to live up to. **I couldn't imagine anyone saying that a white doctor could not treat a black patient, or a white mechanic could not work on a black person's car**. The teaching profession is one of the noblest professions we have. To suggest that persons in that profession could not offer their professional services to people outside of their race is a terrible insult to the profession. I think too much of my profession and my professionalism to even entertain such a thought. No teacher or promoter of education should be advocating that white teachers should not be teaching black children.

Another closely related question I get from white teachers is, **"Can a white teacher teach black children effectively?"** My answer to that question is, "That depends on whether you are an effective teacher." **If you are an effective**

teacher and are teaching any children effectively, you can be an effective teacher to black children. Black children are not black children; they are children who are black. I suppose we could get into a discussion of what comes first, the color, or the child. I am convinced that it is the child. **The child is more a child than he or she is a color**. <u>There are some things that are universally true about children; good teachers relate to those things and therefore, relate to all children</u>. White teachers who are effective teachers of other children can also be effective teachers of black children.

This is not to say that black children will not offer some challenges. Whenever we broaden our horizons we are challenged. But this is a challenge that is good for white teachers. If you meet the challenge posed by teaching black children, it will make you a more effective teacher of all children.

A word should be said here about what is meant by effective teaching. So often black children are allowed to attend predominantly white schools and leave there after three or four years with few or no credits and very little positive information to show for their stay. This occurs in part because white teachers and administrators do not effectively teach and supervise black children. They often retreat and let black children have their way. They often let black children redefine the white schools. In essence, black children turn white schools into black schools, while white teachers and administrators stand back and let them. That is not effectively teaching black children. **Effective teaching would require that black children learn from a core curriculum and that that curriculum would be taught in such a way that they could learn. It would also mean demanding from black children the behavior and commitment that would lead to success in school. This would require commitment from the home, the administration, the child, and the teacher, just as it does with children of any other color.**

However, one thing that the effective teaching of black children does not require of white teachers is that white teachers somehow become black. One of the questions I get that is related to this question is, **"Do I have to act black?"** Personally, I don't know what acting black is. I know a great number of black people and none of them act just like the others. **Black people come in all kinds of shades and varieties of personalities and life styles. There is no one black way of acting or thinking. One of the great challenges white teachers face in teaching black children is to accept them as you find them and guide them to where you think they should be**. If the white teacher is to accept black children as black, they should demand that the black children accept them as white. They both act the way their cultures and circumstances taught them to act. White teachers should not compromise themselves and their profession by trying to be anything they are not. Children want adults to be genuine. You can't be a genuine adult by trying to act like a child, and you can't be a genuine person of one color if you spend your time trying to act as if you are another color. White teachers are asked to be genuine with black children and to require that black children be genuine with them and with themselves. Genuineness will show through color.

White teachers can effectively teach black children if they have the courage to confront them. **Education is confrontation with ignorance. There is almost always a clash when ignorance is challenged and enlightenment is presented.** Many white teachers are not comfortable confronting black children, and understandably so, since they are often not backed by administrators at their schools, or the black community. But one can not be an effective teacher if he or she does not confront ignorance. **Children who are violating rules must be confronted, or they will think their behavior is appropriate and will continue that behavior and expect it to lead to the rewards they seek.** White teachers and white administrators do black children a great injustice when they allow them to practice self-defeating behaviors and do not confront them. That which will not be accepted outside of the schools in legitimate society should not be accepted inside of the schools. To accept such behavior from black children is to set them up for failure. White teachers can effectively teach black children if they demand from black children the behavior and the performance that will be necessary for them to succeed beyond the school.

This brings me to another often asked question: **"What should my expectations be for black children?"** This question annoys black teachers. To them it is unthinkable that a teacher would ask such a question about black children. But I understand the question and think it is quite appropriate. **We teach by permission.** Those of us who work with other people's children do what we feel the parents of those children approve of us doing. I get along well with the students and parents in my district because I share basically the same values they share and want primarily the same things for their children that they want for them. We work with each other in preparing the children for those things. **I have never doubted that the parents of my students wanted me to teach them the core curriculum and demand that they do their best in it. Beyond that, I have never**

doubted that the parents of my students wanted me to teach those students to be socially mature, ethically sound, responsible in their group interaction and personal behavior, and to be good citizens. I feel I have their permission to teach these things and I get ongoing feedback from them that suggests to me that I am accurate in my assumptions. Furthermore, I have seen nothing coming out of the white community that would suggest that I am wrong in my assumptions. So, I feel comfortable with my assumptions and I act on them daily.

The white teacher, on the other hand, does not always feel she has permission from black parents to teach, correct, and guide black children. Since whites generally have little contact with black people in their daily lives, much of what they see of the black community comes to them by way of the evening television news. And the messages whites get about blacks from the news speak of the very worst in the black community. Consequently, they do not know what to expect from black children and they do not know what black parents will support them in doing with black children. **So, it is natural for white teachers to ask a black educator, "What should my expectations be for black students?" When they ask that of this educator, my answer to them is, "The very best in everything."**

White teachers should expect black children to come to class on time and prepared to work. They should expect them to be well disciplined and courteous. They should expect them to be academically motivated and prepared to do the work on the level of the class in which they have them. They should expect them to do all of the things the other students do, and to do them just as well. This should be the expectation, even if the teacher knows that the child has legitimate reasons why he can not easily live up to the teacher's expectations. The teacher should uphold these expectations and challenge the child to live up to them regardless of how difficult or unlikely it will be for him to attain them. Expectations go a long way in inspiring performance. If the child falls short in his performance it should never be because the teacher fell short in her expectations.

Another question that is posed to me frequently by white teachers concerns the teaching of values. **White teachers want to know whether they should impose their values upon black children**. This issue of values is a problem in public schools because of the mixture of ethnic groups in the classroom.

When I was in school there was never a discussion of whether the teacher should impose her values on me. It was assumed that the teacher's values were my values. All of us were black. All of us were Christian, and mostly Baptist. And all of us came from similar backgrounds and saw ourselves as having a similar destiny. The issue of values was a clear cut issue. The parents began teaching values at home and the teachers continued to teach and enforce those values at school.

Now that our schools are integrated and black teachers are teaching white children, and white teachers are teaching black children, and each community claiming to have different values and different goals for itself, there is controversy over values. It, like many other issues in education, is an empty controversy. **There should be no controversy over the teaching of values. White teachers should not have to be uneasy about teaching values to black children**.

To begin with, the values that matter have no color. **White teachers have no values that are the properties of white teachers, just as black people have no values that are the properties of black people**. The values on which western civilization was built and is maintained are neither black nor white. They are the combined and refined ways of the western world. They are the best of what we have preserved that enabled us to survive and thrive as a people. They are preserved for us basically in the Bible, our sacred documents, and our treasured literary works. They have been adopted by the country and they are what enabled this country to prosper as a civilized nation. To reject these values is to reject the best from our past and to invite doom on our civilization. **Every teacher should teach the values that developed the country. Every countryman should want to embrace these values. Without them we would be nothing. To teach kids other things and leave out values is to simply empower them to do harm to the country**. An old black preacher said of such people, they only become "clever devils." It is necessary for the white teacher, and indeed for any teacher, to be in touch with the home and share these values with the parents so the teacher and parent can support each other in the teaching of shared values.

One of the specific values white teachers are frustrated with is the value black children place on retaliation rather than mediation. White teachers want to know what they can do about black children fighting. I have been told by some white teachers that they have stopped black children from fighting only to be told by the children that their parents instructed them to hit back if they are ever hit. In cases like this the teacher might find it necessary to call the parent and explain the school's policy to the parent and explain how that policy works best for the school and country. It might also be necessary to explain to the parent that the values of this country must be embraced if education is going to pay off for the child. At any rate, and whatever has to be done, the white teacher and every teacher need to teach values. Without such values education is dangerous.

The first time I heard the next question, I thought it would be a 'one time only' question that was asked by that one teacher in that one place, and would never come up again. I was wrong. It has come up so many times since. In fact, I almost never have a question and answer session with white teachers that the following question does not come up. The question is, **"Should I correct black children's speech?"** I am mildly amazed at how often this question comes up. Many white teachers have a real problem with correcting the speech of black children. They are told that there is such a thing as black culture, and speech is a part of that culture. There have even been books written to explain and legitimize the speech patterns of black people. Some Blacks have gotten quite a bit of mileage and money out of this argument. I attended a work shop recently on black speech. So, I guess I should not have been so surprised at this question, and should not be surprised that it comes up so frequently in my question and answer sessions.

My answer to that question is that America has one standard English language. It is the language of commerce. It is the language used on Wall Street. It is the language used in corporate America. It is the language taught in our colleges and universities. And it is the only language that teachers are certified and authorized to teach, and should be the only language they promote in the classroom. If children have a language they use outside the classroom and it works for them, that is fine. But teachers are paid to teach the standard usage in the school, and they should always challenge students to hold to that standard. Blacks children should be no exception. **In fact, black children, more than any other children, are judged by their language, therefore, they should be taught to use the very best grammar.** I know that many Blacks disagree with me on this issue, arguing that these children come from neighborhoods where standard English is not used and they feel put down when their language is denounced. There is a way to correct without denouncing. **Teachers are to correct the incorrect grammar of the student and require standard usage. Education is more about where people are going than it**

is about where they came from. Children go to school because of their future, not because of their past. Education shows most prominently in a person's use of the language. All teachers should correct all improper language usage in all their students. White teachers should stand fast in this effort with black students regardless of the resistance they may get at the time. After all, education is confrontation with ignorance. You can take comfort in the fact that the students will remember you, respect you, and thank you for that which you do for them that turns out to be to their benefit.

"Why are black girls so loud and what can be done about it?" This questions always gets a chuckle from white and black teachers. We all wonder what can be done about loud black girls. I usually tell teachers who ask this question that volume is usually set according to the sounds around you. If you are in a loud environment you have a tendency to raise the volume of everything you want to hear. The inner city environment can be a very loud environment at times, and girls who want to be heard over the other noises must talk louder than those noises. **I also explain that part of the loudness of black girls comes from their need to assert themselves in an environment where they have been the underdogs for so long.** Another reason they are loud is because they do not know how inappropriate and ineffective their loudness is in a disapproving environment. Teachers should let black girls know in no uncertain terms that their loudness is not necessary and is unbecoming to educated, refined women. For a thorough discussion of black females, I refer teachers to the essay in this book on **EDUCATING AT-RISK BLACK FEMALES.**

There are other questions that white teachers ask about black students that are not as frequently asked as these, but they are all given the same serious attention. I think every question is an important one, for they are indications of persons seeking a better understanding of children they want to help.

I usually close these sessions by telling teachers to remember that beyond their blackness, black children are just children. They have had some experiences that may be unique to them and that has caused them to shape some attitudes that are unique to them, but beyond those experiences and attitudes they are children trying to find their way to brighter tomorrows. And it is those tomorrows that we must keep in mind when we work with these students. What kind of tomorrows are we preparing them for? When we have questions about our policies or regulations with black children, we should be guided by what kind of tomorrows we envision for them. We should consider where we are preparing these kids to go, rather than focusing on where they came from.

One's approach to teaching is impacted by his vision of his student's future. **When I look at black children I picture persons on their way to some of the best jobs and positions in America. I picture men and women running successful households and rearing good children. I picture them being politicians, and community leaders. I picture them preaching great sermons, and singing great songs. I picture them playing basketball in the N. B. A., and football in the N. F. L. I picture them doing brain surgery and designing buildings for the twenty-first century. I picture them hosting the Tonight Show and starring in soap operas. I picture them being architects and custodians. I picture them teaching school and building houses. I picture them being all the good things that I can imagine. I even picture some of them doing the unimagined. I keep the picture of what I want black children to be in my mind. So when I see them doing anything that I think will keep them from being what I picture them being, I intervene and try to redirect them toward the behaviors and practices that will lead to the pictures I have of them.**

When white teachers ask me about black children, I answer them based upon the goals I have for black children, and the hope I have that they will aspire to those goals and achieve them. I hope that white teachers will buy into these goals. **I hope that white teachers will come to see black children as persons being prepared for the same kinds of futures for which the white children are being prepared. When they do they will hold black children to the same high standards of behavior to which they hold white children. When they treat a black child the same as they treat a child whom they are trying to prepare for the highest of goals, they will not have so many second thoughts about their treatment of black children. And they will not have to ask some of the questions I have addressed here.**

"Education is never complete, and is seldom begun until man realizes the significance of it."

W. L. Jenkins

How The Schools Have Failed The Black Poor

Public schools have been highly criticized for the past several years. The critics cite falling test scores and rising drop out rates as evidence of the decline of public education. Public schools deserve some criticism, but not the blanket indictment they are receiving from some of their harshest critics. Having spent most of my life in public schools, I will concede that they are not perfect, but I can assure you that they are not nearly as bad as their critics would have us believe. Furthermore, the students who enter the schools prepared to learn are being better educated today than ever before.

The biggest problem in public schools today is with those students who come to the schools lacking the discipline and the values that those whom the schools have helped so much in the past have had. Probably the largest segment of that group that the school is not effectively educating are the children of the poor, especially the black poor. And in spite of all of the efforts at educating them, the black poor remain at the bottom of the educational and economic ladder. If public schools deserve criticism, it is for what they have done or failed to do with the black poor, which will be the focus of this effort.

The social thrust for the last thirty years has been to educate the poor and move them up from poverty. The effort worked with other groups, but it has not worked with the black poor. **Even after years of integrating many of them into some of the best schools and school districts, the black poor have shown very little economic improvement.**

Regardless of where they have gone to school, large numbers of the black poor have not been affected by education. Those who go to predominantly white schools are dropping out of those schools at the same, or higher rate than are the poor blacks who go to schools in all black neighborhoods. Whatever schools have been able to do to help other groups improve their economic condition, it has not worked for the black poor. And the schools are being blamed.

The lack of progress of the black poor is an American dilemma, and no one person or group is to blame for that lack of progress. Many institutions have participated in the black poor's stagnant status as permanent occupants of the bottom of the economic heap. The government, with all of its social programs, has been the biggest culprit. But the schools have had a part also, and should be held accountable for the part they have played. Education has not helped the black poor because it has not been given to them in its undiluted, uncompromising, powerful, demanding, and life changing form and dosage. **What the black poor has received at schools has not been an education, but a placebo, with all of the appearances of an education, but none of the affects. In short, the schools have failed the black poor.**

The school's failure to the black poor has not been intentional or malicious. It has been done with the best of intentions and goodwill. But those intentions and goodwill have not led to good results. There are several actions that we have taken, or not taken, in our attempts to educate the black poor that have been very detrimental to them. I will explore these steps in the hope that educators will learn from their mistakes and mend their ways in time to save what is yet salvageable among the black poor. What follows is what I see as our failures to the black poor.

To begin with, **we have not made clear to the poor the relationship between education and economic well being.** There is a reason why educated people are very seldom poor, and why uneducated people almost always are. Educated people may have poor beginnings, but they seldom remain poor after they become educated. But the ignorant will usually remain poor regardless of how much money passes through their hands. There are uneducated poor people who make as much or more money as educated people, but the uneducated, even though they may make a lot of money, often remain poor. To the contrary, people almost always improve economically once they become educated. The reason is simple, education is not just about how much money one makes, education is about the values and life style one embraces.

The primary functions of education are to teach people to appreciate appropriate values and to embrace a life style commensurate with those values. A secondary function of education is to develop students' skills and capacities so they can function productively in, and contribute to a society where those values are the dominating values that drive the society. Ultimately, it is people's values and the way they live that improve their lives economically, not the kinds of jobs they have or the amount of money they earn.

Middle class status is defined more by values and life style than by income. Middle class people seek to become educated because they value what they can do with an education, not just because of what they can get from it. With an education people can promote the kind of society they value. The first colleges and universities in this country were established to prepare people to be leaders in the church and commonwealth. In other words, to promote the things they valued. For that reason, much of the early curriculum was centered around values: Philosophy, Religion, Ethics, and the Social Sciences. It was those values that produced that which is best in our society even today. So, of course, those who embrace the values upon which this society is built will do better here than those who denounce those values. To let people go through school thinking they are being educated and headed for a better life while ignoring the values that would lead to that better life, is to fail them. This is one way in which the schools have failed the black poor. We have let them assume they were educated without having the values that serve as the foundation for education. So their poverty persists and they are perplexed.

Furthermore, we have failed to explain to the black poor why they are poor, that their poverty has more to do with their values and choices than with anything else. Fundamental to changing any condition and keeping it changed, is knowledge of how the condition developed in the first place. It is a poor doctor who will not tell his patient the cause of his ills. **As educators, we have done everything about black poverty except tell black people the truth about its causes.** We have remained silent as black politicians blamed slavery and racism. We have talked about an uneven playing field, we have pointed to a lack of affirmative action, and we have created reason after reason why black poor people are, and remain poor. <u>We have done everything except to tell the black poor that much of their poverty results from their life styles, and that they will remain poor as long as they embrace those life styles that are keeping them poor</u>. Since practically all of the children of the poor go to public schools, it is the challenge of the schools to lift them out of poverty, if they can indeed be lifted at all. It is the challenge of the schools to address those life styles that keep people poor, or at the very least tell them that their efforts are futile as long as they avoid adopting the behaviors that will lift them.

<u>Part of the the school's failure with the black poor is not simply that they have not taught them the values they should embrace in order to be successful, but that they</u>

have not demanded compliance, and they have allowed the children of the poor to remain in school whether they complied or not. The school has allowed and contributed to the poor believing that the experience they were having at school would work without the values they needed. The schools have further participated in the delusion by allowing the children to be successful at school for things they will never be successful for beyond school, thus strengthening their resolve in the convictions that are leading to their doom.

Whenever large numbers of students succeed in school only to fail in society, there is serious cause to question what they are doing in school and/or what they are being required to do in society. Great numbers of the black poor are dropping out of school, but a larger number graduate and never have productive lives beyond high school. They return to communities that remain the poorest, dirtiest, bleakest, and most crime ridden communities in our country, never to escape again. And because they thought they were headed somewhere that they never made it to, they are usually angry because of the false promises they feel were made to them by society.

Educators should tell the black poor plainly and simply that one does not improve his plight simply by getting an education, improvement comes when one becomes an educated person. Education promotes a set of values, and a style of living that goes with those values. Individuals who do not embrace the values and the life style that goes with them will not be nearly as successful as those who do. Educators should not keep quiet on the issues that matter in the economic development of black people. Educators should not keep quiet about teenage pregnancy and life styles and life choices that doom a people to poverty. It is not racist or insensitive to tell black girls that sixteen year old mothers and fathers can not rear children who will be able to compete with the children of more mature, better educated, and more economically stable parents. Educators need to stop worrying about political correctness and start concerning themselves with the survival of a race. It is the survival of a large segment of the black race that is at stake. And until the schools stand up to the children of the poor and tell them the things that will make a difference in their lives, the children of the poor will continue to go through our schools and return to their lives of poverty. And until we confront them, we are failing them.

Instead of confronting the black poor, the schools have lowered their standards and accepted, and even encouraged mediocrity from

them. One does not improve the plight of a people by lowering standards, but by insisting that the people reach up to the standards.   My black teachers in the South always insisted that I went higher than the standards. They thought that meeting the standards would only guarantee that we stayed where we were, behind. But going beyond the standards would give us a chance to move a little closer to those who were at the top.   So they set high standards and encouraged us to reach for them. They did not come down to us, they challenged us to come up to them, and to go beyond them. By doing so, the race advanced.

The children of the black poor today are not being similarly challenged. Academic mediocrity is accepted from them, even expected and encouraged. In many of our schools, the only area in which black children are expected to perform with excellence is in sports. They are expected to overcome any obstacle to be great athletes, but no obstacles is too small to be used by them and some of their teachers as an excuse for academic mediocrity.

If black children are to be successful in life beyond school, they must be challenged to do their best in school.   In life beyond the schools, black children will have to compete with the best for the best, and if they want the best they should be willing to produce the best. They will only be able to give their best if they have some practice at doing so. That practice should come in school. Schools that allow black children to graduate without challenging them to do their best are setting them up for failure after high school.

I find it appalling that so many black children at my school come to their senior years either with not enough credits to graduate, not a high enough G.P.A., or not a sufficient knowledge base to succeed at an academically rigorous college or university. The counselors and teachers do not tell them that the courses they are taking, and the effort they are putting forth, and the grades they are making, will not get them to their expressed goals. It is as if the counselors believe the black students when the students tell them that they are going to college on academic scholarships while making mostly D's and C's in high school. Where do teachers and counselors think these colleges are located? Why are black students not told that there are no reputable colleges that are giving academic scholarships to students who are barely passing in high school. And why are the academic scholarship requirements for black students usually lower than those for white students? It seems that we have all bought into some kind of conspiracy to keep the black poor at the bottom. No wonder they blame society for their problems. The schools should not participate in the delusions of poor blacks. Educators should tell them the truth and insist that they act on that truth while they are in school. Anything less is failing them.

Schools have failed the black poor by catering to the worst among the black poor rather than challenging the best among them. It baffles and angers me that school officials, especially white school officials, are so willing to spend great amounts of time trying to change the worst black students, while spending so little time working with the best black students. I sometimes think that in the case of white educators, they have such low expectations for black people that they think all of them are criminals, and saving the bad ones is the justifiable mission of anyone who works with blacks. But the fact is, that even among the black poor, most of the children are decent children who need only structure, direction, and challenge to become successful. However, they will never get that structure, direction and challenge while most of the educator's time is spent working with students who will not heed the very best efforts at instruction.

In the plight of black people, there is a sad history of the entrenched truant destroying the opportunities of those who mean well and would do well if given a chance. Too many schools fail to give the good black children a chance to do well since they spend so much time working with the bad ones. By doing so, they continue to allow the bad ones to destroy the opportunities of the good ones. The schools fail the poor when they cater to the worst black children and reinforce behaviors that are self defeating. The schools should demand from the black poor the behaviors that will lead to success in the broader community, and severely penalize any behaviors that will not lead to the goals of education. To do otherwise, is to fail in our attempts to help black children.

When teaching poor black children the schools have focused too much on the superficial, and not enough on the meaningful. Black people have been the victims of more meaningless educational games than any other people in this country. We develop numerous wasteful and useless programs at the expense of teaching black children from a demanding and relevant curriculum. We take black children out of class for useless programs in cultural diversity, conflict mediation, and any fad that comes along that can look good on paper as something we are doing with our minority population. In the meantime, these children are missing out on the curriculum, which should be their reason for attending school in the first place. The irony of the 'pull outs' for special programs is that the lessons these students are supposed to learn in these special programs would be learned in their classes if the classes were properly taught and the students properly applied themselves. How is it that our white children are expected to succeed without these special programs if such programs are vital to the success of students? To the contrary, these programs have little value and are given to blacks simply to satisfy their need to address a superficial cultural allegiance that does them more harm than good.

The schools have given in to the poor children rather than demand that the children change their ways and adopt the patterns of those who are successful. The need to be politically correct and the fear of offending any of the poor are destroying the chances of poor children to receive an education in our public schools. It puzzles me how a controlling majority can abandon all common sense in their efforts to appease a powerless minority.

I often ask white people why are they afraid to confront poor black people in their reckless behavior. Most of them say that they are afraid of being called racists. White people can not avoid being called racists by the group of blacks who are calling them racists, just as blacks who stand up to this same group can not avoid being called "Oreos," "Sell Outs," and "Uncle Toms." I understand that as a black man. It comes with the territory. But I insist on telling the truth as I understand it. As an educator, I have an obligation to confront ignorance. And as a black man I have an obligation to tell black children the truth that will lead to productive futures.

But too many people back down from the black poor. Too many teachers allow the children of the black poor to call the shots and seal their doom. Some of the black children I teach accuse me of being harder on them than I am on white children. They say that I embarrass them and put them down in front of white children. They say that I do not like them, and some probably say that I am a "sell out." They say these things the first few weeks they are in my class, but by the time the semester ends, I am almost always their favorite teacher. And more black students return to my school to visit me than return to visit all of the other teachers combined. Many of them continue to be friends of mine to this day, and they tell me that I made the difference in their lives by saving them from themselves. However, these same students have very cruel things to say about the teachers and administrators who were willing to let them practice behaviors that were to their detriment. After they leave school, most of the black children can clearly see how the schools failed them. If the children can see how schools are failing the black poor, certainly we ought to be able to see it. And when we see it we should stop it.

The schools' failure with the black poor does not stop with the children, it extends to their parents. Schools have allowed poor parents to be educational free loaders by not requiring that they take an active part in their children's education. **Of all of things that schools have done to the black poor, the worse may well be encouraging the parents of poor children to believe that their children can get a quality education without the parents' participation. The black poor have been allowed to send their children to school with no parental involvement while all the time being assured that their children would get a quality education.** Quality education is most often achieved through parental involvement. Involvement of parents requires commitment from parents.

Some school districts have gone to the extreme of providing black parents with transportation to parent meetings, and having meetings in their neighborhoods in order to get them to attend. On the surface this sounds like wonderful gestures on the part of the school. But in fact, its nonsense. **The black parents who claim they can not get to the school once a year because it is too far away, often go much farther to shopping malls and gambling boats weekly.** If parents valued their children's education, and were told straightforward that their children would not get an education without their involvement, they would get involved or accept the consequences of not being involved. And they would have no grounds on which to blame the school when those consequences were undesirable. When school officials claim to be able to achieve a quality educational outcome for poor children without the cooperation and involvement of their parents, they are failing the black poor.

Ultimately, The school's failure to the black poor comes down to leadership. The schools have failed the black poor by failing to provide them with the leadership that would improve their condition, and failing to demand that they follow established principles that have been proven to lead to success. If it is bad for the blind to follow the blind, it is worse for the sighted to follow the blind. When it comes to the education of black children, those who know have followed those who didn't know. School officials have allowed the black poor to set their own agenda, while ignoring the agenda that would improve their lives. School officials have not demanded very much of the black poor. They have not demanded that the children obey the rules. They have not demanded that the academic focus be maintained. They have not demanded that excellence be pursued, and they have not demanded that those who know take the reigns and lead.

It should be clear to school officials that if the poor knew how to change their condition, they would. And since they don't know how to change their plight, those who do know should demand that those who don't know, follow those who do. That would require that school officials stand up to the poor and tell them that the school will not be a partner to their self delusion and their self destruction.

People who subscribe to education should be required to take the medicine prescribed by educators. If they refuse to take the medicine, the educators should distance themselves from them, for their refusal to get better casts a shadow of suspicion on the profession. That shadow of suspicion is now engulfing the public schools in America. Since the patient will not take the medicine and get better, people are saying that the medicine is weak. But those of us who are in education know that the medicine is strong. It is improving the lives of millions daily. But it can not improve the lives of those who will not take it. Educators should demand that the medicine be taken or that the patient leaves the premise. We have not demanded that the black poor take our medicine, and we have not demanded that they leave the premise. By letting the poor hang around and not make progress, we have given people the impression that the problem is with the school.

The main problem with the school is that it has allowed the black poor to remain there and not demand of them the changes that would improve their lives. We have failed to provide them with the leadership that would make their conditions better. And there is no excuse for such a failure. And even more inexcusable is the fact that we are continuing to fail the black poor. They come to the schools, set the agenda, concern themselves with everything except education, and eventually leave just as lost as they were when they arrived. They return to their neighborhoods and to the streets, as desperately poor and ignorant as they were when they entered the school. And the schools are being blamed for their condition. And the schools have a weak defense. And we will not be able to defend ourselves against the criticism that is being leveled against us until we stand up to the poor and demand that they buy in or get out. The poor should want to buy in even more than we want them to; it is only our reputation that is at stake, it is their survival.

"Let a new earth rise. Let another world be born. Let a bloody peace be written in the sky. Let a second generation full of courage issue forth; Let a people loving freedom come to growth. Let a beauty full of healing, and a strength of final clenching be the pulsing in our spirits and our blood. Let the martial songs be written, let the dirges disappear. Let a race of men now rise and take control."

Margaret Walker

Understanding And Educating
Inner City Black Children

When searching for a title for this book I tried to think of one that would best describe my objectives and my hopes for writing it. The title, <u>UNDERSTANDING AND EDUCATING AFRICAN AMERICAN CHILDREN</u> is a simple title but it says best what my purpose was for compiling the essays that make up this book. Over the last two decades the children we teach in the public schools have changed drastically, and the problems the classroom teacher faces have increased significantly in number and kind. So we greatly need more information about the children who bring us these problems. The students who account for a large number of the problems in today's public schools are inner-city black children with community and cultural baggage that make it hard for them to fit socially into the school and be successful.

One of the major fears of young teachers is having to work with inner city black children. I understand the teachers' fears. Human beings fear the unknown, and much of the fear of city children and of teaching them comes from not knowing them and not knowing what to expect from them. Yet, we have the responsibility of teaching them, even of changing them.   In the last decade, however, we have not been very successful at teaching or changing inner-city black children. Attempts at educating these children have been disastrous. Both their neighborhood schools and suburban schools have had dismal results from their attempt to educate inner city black children. Program after program have met with disappointment. We mounted a monumental effort but have very little to show for it.

We have not made progress in our efforts to educate inner city children partly because we have ignored the obvious and sought complicated answers to simple questions. The problems in education today are much simpler than experts would have us believe. Experts have to justify their expertise by claiming things are too complicated for non- experts to understand, that we therefore need these experts to explain the issues to the rest of us.

Too often the experts who tell us about inner city black children do not know much about these children. **Many of the experts live in lofty suburban areas and see black children only on the evening television news. Other experts rely upon what they remember about the neighborhoods and black people from decades ago**. Still others are so busy pushing vested interests and political agendas that their information is slanted to fit those interests and agendas. One is left with very few people who actually have the insight and intelligence to understand, and the courage and integrity to say what makes educating inner city children so difficult, which was my objective for writing this book.

My connection to and association with these children over the years have given me a unique insight into them and their environment. I live and have always lived among black people. I know first hand of the cultural, political, social, and economic influences that contribute to their being the way they are. I not only know them, but I also know their parents and their grandparents. So I know where they are and where they've been; I know what they are and what they can become. I watched them become what they are; and I urge them to become what I know they can be. I have seen what they can be, and I share my vision of what they can be with them, and those who teach them. For neither they nor their teachers know their true potential. Their true potential is lost in their present stagnant condition, a condition that renders them unteachable beings who come to school with attitudes, behaviors, and life-styles that make it very difficult for them to succeed. In fact, they come to school programmed for failure. Yet, I believe we can teach them in spite of themselves, and reprogram them for success.

Black children's greatest enemy in the classroom is not their poverty, their history, racism, a white curriculum, or a teaching core that does not understand them. The children who fail in school today do so more because of their own attitudes than because of anything else. Black children are no exceptions. Many inner city black children come to school with a cluster of attitudes that make educating them very difficult, if not impossible.

We recognize the importance of attitude in other areas of life. We know how important attitude is in sports, medicine, business, and just about every endeavor, but we have ignored attitude as it pertains to the education of inner-city children. We have placed the responsibility for educating them on everybody except them. It is now time for us to look at them and their attitudes, and to accept the fact that if we want to change them, we must first change their attitudes.

Two cautions I would like to state at the outset for those who will read this book or essay with political agendas. This is not about politics or race; it is about education. This is not about whether the children are justified in having the attitudes they have, or whether the things they base the attitudes upon are true or false. This is about how the attitudes are preventing them from learning what is being taught in schools. Educators know what attitudes complement the educational process. They also know what attitudes block their efforts. **As an educator, I can assure you that inner city black children are hampered in their efforts to get an education more by their attitudes than they are by anything else.** And I am further convinced that we will not make much progress in educating them until their attitudes are compatible with the educational goals they seek. And attitude is something they can change.

Another word of caution, though these characteristics or attitudes are seen in many inner city black children, they are not present in all inner city black children. One of the most amazing things about black city people is that some of them can live in very destructive environments and are seemingly unaffected by those environments. Some of the most gentle black people live in some of the roughest neighborhoods. Some very honest black people live in neighborhoods infested with crime. Some very positive and hopeful black people live in some very depressed areas. **In all of the bad neighborhoods where blacks live some very good black people live there also.** It is for such people that I write and hope. For they are left out of our strategies to save the black community. They need to be saved from that element of the black community that is lost. **These people and their children are brushed over in our mad rush to reach those who are running from our grasp, those with the attitudes.** Having said that, I wish to return to those students with the attitudes.

The black inner city children who fail in school often share common attitudes that are readily recognizable. **The first recognizable attitudes these persons have in common is their attitude toward America.** Many black children have the attitude that they are not full American citizens, and that belief contributes to their less than enthusiastic embracing of education. They associate American education with American institutions and values, and American interests and jobs. **They think American education is about America, and since they don't see themselves as Americans, they halfheartedly pursue their education.**

A child who does not think he is a full citizen will not enthusiastically embrace an educational system designed to empower people to use their citizenship. Black city children have all kinds of illogical notions about their citizenship and their relationship to the country-- and understandably so. They are told that they are victims of slavery and are hardly any better off now than their fore parents were in slavery. Their entertainment is often about their mistreatment. The theme of much of their music-- particularly, Rap music-- and many of their movies is their exploitation. Meanwhile, they do not see many successful black Americans who are proud of their American citizenship. **So these black children conclude that they are not Americans. This is an attitude that has a negative affect on their schooling and on practically every aspect of their lives.**

Closely linked to unsuccessful black children's denial of their citizenship is their over zealous allegiance to poverty and the life--styles of the poor. **Black inner city children think it is normal for blacks to be poor, and in accepting that normalcy, they embrace and accept a lifestyle of poverty**. They think that most black people are poor, and that those who are not poor acquired their money by selling out the blacks who are poor. They think that their blackness requires an allegiance to the poor, and to comply with this allegiance they embrace the ways of the poor. By doing so, they insure for themselves a life of poverty. It is difficult to get poor children to abandon their life styles of poverty because they see abandoning such life styles as turning their backs on other poor people. And those poor people are quick to remind anyone who tries to change, that he is a sell out. **Whenever a black child tries to cooperate with the teachers and take advantage of the opportunities of his citizenship, the other blacks denounce him and try to make him feel that he is being disloyal to the black race**.

Many black children are intellectually conditioned to embrace the beliefs, behaviors, and people that are bad for them. Consequently, their lives are laden with contradictions. They look up to the wrong people and down on the wrong people. **They do all the wrong things in their effort to get where education is designed to take them. The boys embrace lifestyles that are anti-social and anti-establishment while going to schools that are designed to teach them the social skills required to join the establishment. Many of the girls start families that insure their poverty while going to schools designed to lift them out of poverty. They do all of these things with the approval of the black poor, and in some cases, the support and protection of the middle class**. It is difficult for teachers to interest children in the curriculum if these children are conditioned to embrace ideas and lifestyles that are opposed to what the curriculum promotes.

Another attitude black children who fail have in common is their preoccupation with white people as their enemy, and their assumption that white people are just as preoccupied with them. Some city blacks think that there is a conspiracy among white people to keep them down. Such thinking keeps many blacks from taking charge of their lives and doing the things they need to do to progress. It also interferes with their ability to let white teachers effectively teach them. **Black children are convinced that white people are not going to let them progress**. They have heard so much about what white people did to blacks and what white people stopped blacks from doing to progress until they are convinced that whatever they do must be done over the objections of whites. They spend an enormous amount of time battling an enemy that exists only in their minds. This takes away from the energy and interest they could give to their academic pursuits.

Along with the attitude that they are being constantly watched and victimized by whites, black children who fail have the belief that whites owe them. It is a contradiction to think that the same white people who are out to do harm to them are going to ever give them anything. But such is the backward thinking of black children and of many black people. Some blacks believe that there is a group of white people who are the descendants of slave owners who are running the country, and that these people have a great deal of money left over from slavery. They further believe that these descendants of slave masters should share with blacks the wealth they have from slavery. Such thinking works against the efforts of education.

Also included in the cluster of attitudes that black children have that contribute to their failure is their arrogance. A necessary quality for would be scholars is humility. Students who feel they are too important to listen to teachers, seldom do. Many of our students are programmed to feel they are too important to humble themselves to educators and the educational process. Achieving the degree of humility necessary for learning is made even more difficult when it is a white teacher attempting to teach a black child. The child's misguided notions about race prevent him from acquiring the humility necessary to accept the help he needs.

Black children need help as much as any children in our schools. If they are to continue to receive that help, they must learn to develop some humility and show some appreciation. Students can't learn very much without humbling themselves to the educational process and feeling appreciation for it.

As if arrogance alone was not bad enough, the black children who are unsuccessful are usually angry. There is an anger in black children and (indeed in the much of the inner-city black community) that lies just beneath the surface and can erupt at any moment. The anger makes teaching them very difficult. When people are angry they are not likely to concentrate on anything other than that which is causing their anger. Children can not concentrate on education when they are angry about other elements of their lives.

Some say that the anger is a natural response to the injustices blacks have suffered in America. If that were true, it would seem that the blacks who have been the victims of the most injustice, the older blacks, would be the ones displaying the most anger. But it is young blacks who are angry. Blacks who grew up in America when there were many more injustices than there are now are not nearly as angry as the younger blacks are today.

<u>The young blacks are not angry because they have been mistreated; they are angry because they have been told they should be angry</u>. They have been programmed into being angry. They have been told that they are victims and that they have been exploited; therefore, they should be angry about their victimization and exploitation. They should be angry, they are told, about their poverty and their unemployment, about their run-down neighborhoods and their ineffective schools. They are told that they should be angry about the quality of their lives, especially when they compare their lives to the lives of white people. Black people are told that just about everything that is wrong with them is caused in part by white people. If I believed this, I would be angry too. **So I understand their anger even though I disagree with the object of their anger, and the reasons for their anger. They are told that they are victims. And in fact, they are victims, but willing victims. They are not victims of white people; black children are victims of the people who are telling them they are victims. They are victims of a philosophy of victimization.** The messages they are getting about their victimization is destroying them. They are taught to see themselves as victims, as powerless pawns in the white man's racist scheme. And as long as they think they are powerless victims, that is all they will ever be. **And powerless people who accept their powerlessness as permanent have no desire to become educated.**

We pursue an education in the first place because we want it to change the outcome of our lives, even determine that outcome. If we believe the outcome has already been determined by a racist system, education becomes irrelevant. So, regardless of the intentions of those who convince black children that they are victims, the end result is black children who do not approach education with the enthusiasm needed for success.

For those who have the attitude that education will not improve their lives, it is a small step for them to conclude that the unacceptable is acceptable for them when it comes to making money. They often try selling drugs and other crimes as vehicles for upward mobility. And in their neighborhoods these criminal exploits are condoned, at least by the people they choose to listen to, and to some degree, outside of their neighborhoods by people who excuse illegal black behavior on the basis of poverty. So black children come to believe that illegal ways of getting money are acceptable for them. They then adopt lifestyles that leave little or no time for educational pursuits.

Not only do these unsuccessful students think education will not make an economic difference in their lives, they think that education is for white people, while sports and other forms of entertainment are the areas in which blacks can excel. In many cases Black children do not excel in education because they do not believe they have any business excelling. They concede intellectual dominance to whites. Black males particularly, often picture themselves as superior athletes and superior entertainers. They sometimes imagine themselves to be slick and cool, even street smart. But it is quite difficult to get them to picture themselves as scholars. They think that scholarship is the property of whites. They have little academic confidence. **In fact, many of them are ashamed of being smart. They are often ridiculed by their peers when they make good grades. They think blacks have no business being scholars. They have been programmed that way. But if black children would pursue academic goals with the same zeal they put forth in their athletic pursuits, they would do as well in their studies as they do in their sports.**

In addition to all of these attitudes there is another I found in most of the students who fail at my school, especially the males. **Black students who fail display the attitude that they, as blacks, do not have to obey the authority of this country.** This attitude seems to be a culmination off all of the others. In other words, it is the ultimate attitude that all of the others lead to. And it does the ultimate harm. To adequately explain how this attitude is developed would require a book, or at the very least, several chapters. I would ask only that you look at the black attitudes toward the Rodney King incident, the O. J. Simpson case, and at Marion Berry's political fortunes and misfortunes. Without addressing the guilt or innocence of any of these people for any of the crimes of which they have been accused, I want to address the attitudes of some blacks. **There are blacks who are willing to overlook anything any black is accused of in America because they allow everything to be distorted by race.** They suffer from what I call the "white right syndrome", the inability to see right and wrong apart from black and white. Black children, reared in this atmosphere, indoctrinated by the ideas of that environment, do not feel they have to obey the just laws of society, particularly laws that were enacted by whites. Such people will only obey out of fear. Since the fear of breaking the law has been removed for many people, they readily break the law because they feel there will be no consequences. And in many cases they are right. Many of the suspensions and expulsions of black children from schools, especially predominantly white schools, stem from those blacks not respecting white people's rules and not fearing white people's authority. So they challenge the rules. And since there is no immediate consequence, they challenge themselves all the way into expulsion, and eventually prison. The stories I could tell about the young men I know, and have known, who could have been helped if I could have convinced them early enough that white people do have the power to enforce all of the laws of America. But it was hard for me to convince them that their lifestyles were bad for them when they were getting away with everything, Just as it is hard for me to convince black children in schools that they are doing wrong when the system allows the wrong they do to pay so well for so long with attention from teachers and administrators and popularity among the students.

There are other attitudes that inner city black children have that contribute to their failure in school, but they are minor compared to the ones I have discussed here. **And even the ones here, taken alone, might not cause a child to be unsuccessful. But clustered together in any child, these attitudes will certainly prevent success in school--and just about anywhere else.** Therefore, if we are to help the children who have these attitudes--and many of the children who fail do have them--we are going to have to change the attitudes.

We will have to teach inner city black children that citizenship is not something that someone gives them, it is something they must claim. No citizen in this country is empowered to give another citizen citizenship. These students should also be taught that if they are willing to denounce their citizenship in the richest country in the world, they are inviting poverty and exclusion. Teachers need strategies that will shape in students the proper attitude toward the country and their place in it.

We should also have strategies to address the other attitudes the inner city black children bring to class that are hindering their progress. We should work with them on their arrogance, their attitudes about being victims, their belief that they should be given a free ride, their hostility, their penchant for embracing life styles that are destructive, and their tendency for developing unproductive allegiances with the poor. We should teach them that education is a result of hard work and that if they worked as hard at academics as they do at athletics, they would shine as bright in class as they do on the court. **For each of the attitudes that blacks have that are keeping them from being successful in class, we should have a teaching strategy to address that attitude and to change it**.

And finally, an effective educational program for black children must include a strategy to get them to see very early in their lives that there are consequences for improper behavior in this country, and that the consequences are serious. Those consequences plague inner city black communities: ignorance, poverty, sickness, crime, confusion, anger, powerlessness, hopelessness, and utter despair. Black children must be taught that much of what is wrong with them and their neighborhoods results from their ignorance and their refusal to listen to and model after the people who have what they want--the middle class.

We must develop a strategy to teach black children that education is not just about what one knows, but about who and what one is. We must teach them that educated people are expected to know and obey the law, that educated people are expected to know and use common courtesies, that educated people attempt to settle disputes without violence, that educated people have respect for people and peoples, property, principles, the past, and all that is precious. Ultimately, we must teach them that the middle class has one very important characteristic in common with gangs: we will not let people in until they indicate their willingness to be like us. We will not require would be members to participate in a drive-by shooting, or to beat up a member of a rival gang; but we will require that they say, "mam," and "sir," to adults, that they are courteous and respectful, that they value the things we have that they want us to give to them, and that they be proper stewards of our materials, values, country and civilization. If they do not indicate that they can handle these stipulations, then, like the street gangs, we turn them down. We will not write recommendations for them. They will not get the good jobs, or live in the good neighborhoods, and they will never be welcome in our company.

This would be quite a message for poor black children to hear, especially if we think that they are ignorant, and weak, and can not handle it. We tell this to our middle class children all the time, and never think we are doing anything wrong. But we don't cater to them the way we cater to the black poor. Could it be that we love our own enough to make them angry in order to make them better? Whatever the reasons, if we want the black poor to assume the status in society that middle class children assume, we must teach the black poor what the middle class children know. They should be taught these things at home, but they are not being taught to them at home. So it falls to the classroom teacher to teach them what they need to know to get an education and benefit from it.

Teachers are challenged to take these children as they are and transform them into what education is designed to make them. We are to do this without very much help from society, without very much help from the parents, and without very much cooperation from the students. This is a difficult task that is made even more difficult by this notion we have that they all must succeed. Black people are the only people in this country for whom no one among them is allowed to fail without there being a historical, political, social or racial explanation given for that failure. Some people are just not going to be successful in school. They are not cut out for that kind of success. Some are going to fail for any one of a thousand reasons that have nothing to do with their color. We must let the ones fail who are determined to fail, and work at saving those who have the capacity and desire to succeed in the schools. And we must never let those who are determined to fail poison the educational environment and cause many to fail who would have been salvaged with proper and timely teaching. And with a better understanding of black children, we can do that proper and timely teaching, and ameliorate this monumental problem.

I know it seems hopeless. I fight the feeling of hopelessness daily.
When I would be consumed by it I call to remembrance a statement I read in a novel when I was in college that says: "where there is life, there is hope for the amendment of life." And these children are still alive, so we must strive to keep hope alive. And though their lives are broken, even shattered, we are in the mending business. We now know what has led to this brokenness, what has shattered their wholeness, and we must meticulously and painstakingly, and with loving care, gather the pieces of their shattered beings and piece by laborious piece, restore them to their health, if we can. We owe them only our best efforts. If we fail we can take comfort in the fact that we tried our best at the only thing that ever had a chance of working. And if we succeed we can celebrate the rest of our lives, for the victory will grow greater with each passing day.

147

No, I have not forgotten where I came from; nor have I forgotten why I left.
W. L. Jenkins

An Intelligent Approach To Black Culture

For some time now I have contemplated writing a piece on black culture, but kept putting it off hoping that the need for such a writing would go away. But like many other things put off with such hope, the need actually grew greater. It reached its peak one Saturday when I went to a conference to hear a renown black educator and author speak on minority culture. She had written a book on the subject and I had been given a copy a few days prior to the conference. Since I had only had a chance to read a few chapters, I did not really understand her point, but hoped to get a clearer understanding from her presentation. It turned out to be a vain hope.

After sitting through over two hours of the writer's presentation, I was more confused than I had been from reading the few chapters of the book that I had read. Neither from her book, nor the lecture could I make much sense of what she was saying about culture, and that which I could make sense of, made no sense to me. She was advocating that educators structure their curriculums and requirements around the cultures of minority students (mainly black) and not hold those students accountable for anything that is not consistent with the way they do things in their culture.

I strongly disagree with that position so when she came to the point where she allowed for questions I asked her to explain how her material was to have practical applications in the classroom. She dismissed the question and proceeded to discuss a lot of abstract nonsense that further convinced me that it was indeed time for me to write something about culture that classroom teachers could understand and apply in their teaching. In the name of culture black children are being allowed to practice behaviors that are preventing them from being properly educated in our schools.

Culture has a place in school, and the culture of children should never be totally ignored. Teachers should respect and appreciate culture, and even use it to teach lessons when it can be done within the context of the curriculum and its goals. But the notion that educators should spend endless hours studying minority culture, and that minority students should be excused from the rigors of academic pursuits on the basis of their culture, is ludicrous and damaging to minority students and the country.

Understanding culture can be a pathway to more effective teaching, however, when too much emphasis is placed on culture, it can be a hindrance to the education of students. All groups have some cultural values and traditions that should be respected and preserved. However, if people hold on to cultural traditions that have outlived their usefulness, it can be an impediment to their progress. Likewise, if they reject parts of their culture that should be preserved, that too can be harmful to them. In some cases, blacks are doing both. Some black educators are promoting aspects of black culture that are detrimental to black people, and are at the same time ignoring elements of black culture that could be a great help to the whole nation.

Culture is impacted by economic and social conditions, political and intellectual forces; and in modern times, technological advances. If a group develop the bulk of their cultural customs under one social condition and are then thrust into a different one; or if technological advances or new knowledge occur that make their cultural practices obsolete, to stay abreast of the times they must put aside some of their cultural practices in favor of newer and better ways of doing things.

In the case of Blacks in America, much of what we call our culture was developed during a time of slavery and oppression, and the way we did things then was based on our condition and a limited knowledge of Western Culture. Even after our ancestors were freed from slavery they were still kept ignorant about what was going on in America and the world. Therefore, our culture from the very beginning was shaped under sub standard and oppressive conditions.

Add to those factors the fact that in the last hundred years we have seen the most dramatic changes in the history of civilization, it becomes obvious what will happen to a people in this culture who insist on clinging to their old ways rather than embracing new ones. Those who are first to embrace the newer and superior ideas and principles become the more advanced, while those who insist on clinging to the old and inferior are left behind. Whether that clinging to the old is a result of pure ignorance concerning the new, or loyalty to their culture, the results are the same.

Unfortunately, many of the behaviors that black people are calling their culture are not a part of black culture at all, but are simply the behaviors of a misguided group of black children who have not been given proper direction and have not embraced the life styles and values of their ancestors. For the most part, they have rejected the best of black culture.

Many of the black children today who are said to be expressing black culture know next to nothing about traditional black culture. They have studied very little, if any, black history. In many instances they have not traveled beyond their neighborhoods, and they are not in touch with any great black traditions. Instead, they copied these behaviors from an entertainment world that knows as little about black culture as they do, and whose main interest is making money by selling garbage to poor black children.

My recollection of black culture is very different from today's young blacks. I remember black people having very strong religious convictions. Practically all of the black people I knew growing up belonged to the church. They were close as a group, and they helped and looked out for each other. The blacks I remember formed societies, worked hard, respected all adults, were very devoted to each other, embraced education, and tried to make sure that life would be better for their children than it had been for them. And contrary to what is commonly promoted today, most black children in those days grew up in two parent families. That is the black culture I remember and my memories go back a half century. It was also the culture of the people from whom I learned my culture, which extends back to slavery.

The sagging pants, the caps, the hoodlum look, the loudness, the disrespect for authority, and the anti-education attitudes that are causing black children to fail in school today are not a part of the black culture I remember. These behaviors have become the culture of the black underclass, and as long as they embrace them they will remain in that underclass. Those who justify such behaviors in the name of culture are doing a great disservice to black children, the black race, and the country.

Black students should not be allowed to fail in school practicing behaviors that they call their culture. Those who are genuinely interested in black children's success should stop advocating that in the name of culture they be allowed to follow practices that hinder their success in school, and ultimately their success in life. They should not be advocating that black children be taught in a different manner from the rest of the students, or that black children have learning styles that are different from the rest of the student populations and that in order to reach them teachers must teach to their learning styles. They should not be advocating that we accept loud black girls and academically tuned out black boys because it is their culture. Much of this talk about poor black children's culture is simply an excuse contrived by middle class blacks because they believe that these black children are never going to fit into middle class society so they make excuses for them before they try.

Culture has to be transmitted. Children don't have a culture until one is passed on to them. Black children could just as easily receive the culture of middle class whites as the culture of poor blacks. Children are the products of culture, not the property of culture. No culture owns them, but any culture can be adopted by them. We should be trying to get black children to adopt a culture that is going to improve their plight rather than condemn them to the bottom of the economic ladder. Why not the culture of Frederick Douglas and George Washington Carver? They were black. Why not the culture of Harriet Tubman and Marion Anderson? Were they not Black? Why not the culture of Charles Drew and Carter G. Woodson? Certainly they were black. Why not the culture of the countless black men and women who have distinguished, and continue to distinguish themselves by practicing those cultural traits that have allowed black people to rise up from slavery to a status of power and distinction in this country? Black people have enough culture that is good and helpful that black children should never have to stoop to behaviors that are bad and demeaning to connect to or express black culture.

In the final analysis, education makes us all new creatures. It gives us an awareness of new things and techniques. Education is forever exploring new information, discounting old myths and lies, and confirming age old truths that are permanent and unalterable. Education is sometimes painful and threatening, but it is always enlightening and enhancing. It would be tragic for any country to allow a segment of its population to be excused from the challenges of education, and thereby cut off from its great benefits in the name of culture. In many instances, black children in our schools are being cut off from the benefits of education while their educators discuss the best cultural approach to teaching them.

Our approach should be to be sensitive to the child's culture, while at the same time giving him the best education possible. All truly educated people have the same culture: living according to the latest research and time tested truths. Black children deserve to have those truths as much as any other children, and their teachers should teach them that embracing new and better ways is not a disrespect to their culture, but a responsibility that they have to themselves. Education is about the best and the latest. When new knowledge proves superior to old ways, old ways ought to be abandoned in favor of the new knowledge.

However, just because a thing is new does not mean that it is better. If an old practice brings better results than a new fad, we should stick with the old practice rather than abandoning it simply because it is old. Cultural practices should be judged by their results; if they bring about the desired results, they should be kept. But if they are causing the people who practice them to be less healthy, less well educated, less familiar with the technology that impacts their lives, and less productive citizens than are other people, those practices, regardless of how dear they are to the people who hold them, should be abandoned.

Interestingly enough, there are many aspects of black culture that black children and the country would do well to hold on to. Black people's devotion to God, family, duty, hard work, and the country, are all qualities that America could stand a healthy dose of. Our propensity to value people more than possessions, and God's will for our lives over our own selfish wills, would be something that would help young black people immensely. However, these are not the cultural qualities that are being promoted by those blacks who think we ought to make allowances for black children's culture. Instead, black students are being allowed and encouraged to destroy their educational opportunities in the name of culture. Those of us who know better need to put a stop to it.

Any practice, cultural or otherwise, that does not lead to the goals of education should be denounced by educators. Middle class blacks should not allow poor black children to reject their education in favor of their culture. The black educator who prompted me to finally write this piece received her education at a predominantly white school, was teaching at a predominantly white university, had sent her daughter to predominantly white schools, made this presentation that I heard at a predominantly white school, and she probably lives in a predominantly white neighborhood. Yet, she is advocating that in the name of culture we allow poor black children to be restricted, to wallow in ignorance, ignore the advances taking place all around them, and to never be allowed entry into mainstream America.

Right thinking people can not allow such an injustice to be perpetrated upon black children. Well meaning educators of all colors must take a stand against this terrible misuse of culture and challenge black children and all children to prepare themselves to live successfully in the twenty first century.

And Let us not be weary in well doing: for in due season we shall reap, if we faint not.

Galatains 6:9

What Black Children Need In Their Teachers

A few years ago I did a lecture at St. Louis University to the students in their education program on the subject: "What Black children need in their teachers." After reading this book up to this point you too might be wondering what black children need in their teachers, and whether you have it. Therefore, I thought that the ideas expressed in that lecture might be a fitting ending for this book. It was awkward for me to give such a lecture since I believe that black children are basically the same as other children and have basically the same needs, and that whatever is true for other children is also true for black children. However, since the education of black children has been such a political and controversial issue, I thought it might be helpful and reassuring for a veteran black educator to reaffirm what black children need in their teachers.

First of all, black children need teachers who are suited for teaching today's children. Many of the teachers entering the classroom today are not cut out for teaching the children of today. Today's students are often very different from students of past years. Since college education programs may do very little to prepare teachers for the reality of today's classroom, some young people finish teaching programs with little understanding of what teaching is like. As a result, many of them leave teaching within five years of entering the profession. They find that they are not right for teaching in today's climate.

How does one know whether he/she is suited for teaching? There is no guaranteed way, but there are some questions that you can ask yourself and the answers will give you a pretty good indication of whether you are cut out for teaching in these times. One of the first questions you should ask yourself is, do I want to teach children, or do I just want to teach the best children? Public schools have very little control over who enrolls in them. If you are not willing to give your best effort at teaching any child, you are probably not suited for teaching today's children, especially those who attend our public schools.

The second question you should probably ask yourself is, "do I care enough about kids and this country to give my life to making them both better?" That is exactly what you will be required to do as a teacher. Teaching is all consuming. It will take your life. You will give a little of your life to each child, each class, each semester, each year in an effort to make every child a better person and America a better place. If you care about such things and bring to that care a passion to pursue them with every child, you are probably cut out for teaching. Black children need you.

Black children need people who are cut out for teaching, for they will test your commitment to teaching and to them every day. If you are weak in your commitment to either, you will give up and give in, and you will be one of those who leave the profession within the first five years. But if you are strong in your beliefs and your commitment, you will hold on and hold out. Black children need teachers who are strong enough and committed enough to stay the course.

In addition to needing teachers who are cut out for teaching, black children need teachers who want to teach them, not the white children who used to attend the school, not even the black children who used to attend the school, but those children who are there staring in the face of the teacher that day; with all of their baggage, all of their hostilities, all of their misgivings about the teacher and education itself, and all of the attitudes that are going to make teaching them difficult.

I visit schools where the student populations and neighborhoods have changed significantly since some of the teachers joined the faculty. Some of the schools have gone from being all white schools to practically all black schools. Some are in neighborhoods that have gone from being mainly middle class to poor. Some of the teachers at these schools teach with the same fervor, passion and dedication that they always brought to their classrooms. But there are others who simply lament the days gone by and look forward to retirement. They may have been effective teachers in the past, but they have no interest in teaching the students who are presently enrolled in their schools. Black students do not need such teachers teaching them.

Black students also need teachers who can relate to their plight, but yet not use their circumstances as an excuse for low expectations and inferior work or behavior. It is difficult to understand what some students are up against when your life is so far removed from their reality. It is difficult to sympathize or empathize with the plight of kids without knowing some of the things that they are experiencing. Some teachers, because they are so far removed from the reality of the children, can't begin to imagine what life is like for them.

Black students need teachers who can understand what they are going through, but they don't need them to use their present circumstances as an excuse for them not doing their work. The fact that the children's plight is bad is greater reason for the teacher to be demanding. If their situations are bad now, they will only be worse for the next generation if the cycle is not broken with the children we see.

Knowing the plight of children should help motivate teachers to help students construct strategies to survive and triumph over their conditions. Knowing what people are going through helps you appreciate and admire their struggle. I have had some students who had it tough. When I found out the extent of their troubles I became more determined to help them. Understanding more about their situations enabled me to help them work out specific strategies to overcome them. Interestingly enough, some of my students who have had the greatest struggles were not black. I have had some white students over the years who had some really heavy burdens to bear, and with the help of caring teachers they overcame them. Today's teachers need to listen to kids and find out a little more about what is going on with them and address some of their hurts as they interact with them. I sometimes write short personal notes on the papers of students who I know are having tough times. Students have a different attitude when they know that the teacher knows and cares about their problems. They are more open and trusting when you start helping them plan a strategy to overcome their situation.

Black children need teachers who care about them personally and are able to communicate that concern as they work with them. Unfortunately, today's students need to believe that the teachers care about them. Even if they are not smart and are not good students, they want to be cared about personally. In fact, the worse they are, the more they need Teachers to care about them. I can't tell you how many kids over the years have told me that I was the only teacher at the school who they felt really cared about them. Some of my most moving moments as a teacher have come when a student has slipped me a note or a Christmas card, or some little token of appreciation and told me that I had shown a concern for him/her that no other teacher had. Even though it feels good to me to be recognized as a caring teacher, I feel badly when kids tell me that I am the **only one who cares**. I try to assure them that most of their teachers care about them, some just have different ways of showing it. Black children need teachers who care about them.

Black Children need teachers who will stand up to them and for them. Teachers who care about black kids need to stand up to them and for them. I could fill several books this size with episodes that have taken place between me and some of those students who finally concluded that I cared about them. Some of the episodes were not very friendly or pretty. However, some were quite hilarious. And once we become friends, my students and I spend many hours laughing and talking about the confrontations we had in our early encounters. They now see those confrontations as evidence of my concern and my unwillingness to stand idly by and watch them destroy themselves without putting up a fight. They saw the fights as a sign of caring.

Today's students will test your resolve. If you are weak and fearful, you will give up and let the children have their way. But you can't let any child have his way if you expect him to fit into society as a responsible citizen. Some black children love to intimidate teachers, especially white teachers. They brag about how they scare white teachers into letting them do whatever they want to do, especially after they accuse white teachers of being racist. These students don't know that they, not their teachers, are the losers in these confrontations. But they are able to get their way temporarily because the teachers do not stand up to them. Black students need teachers who know what's good for the students and insist that they do it.

In addition to standing up to them, black children need teachers who will also stand up for them. Their teachers need to stand up to those who are advocating things for black students that are not in their best interest. Some blacks want black children to be able to practice behaviors that are counter productive. I have been in meetings where blacks advocated things for black students that were senseless, and white educators who knew better said nothing. I suppose the white educators felt that blacks had more right to make decisions in behalf of black children than did whites. I strongly disagree. Black people should not be given license to dig the graves of black children just because they are black. I do not remain silent when white people give my white students bad advice, and white teachers shouldn't stand by and let black teachers or black civic leaders give black children bad advice. Black students need all of their teachers to stand up against the insanity that is pushed toward them in the name of education. Children don't know enough to advocate for themselves, they need knowledgeable and caring adults to advocate for them, parents and teachers. In the absence of parents, teachers are the children's best advocates. Therefore, black students need teachers who will stand against the forces that would destroy their chances of having a quality education.

One final statement about standing up to and for black children. I understand how difficult and threatening it can be, especially for white teachers, and especially for young non-tenured teachers, to get involved in controversy and conflict about black students. There are some blacks on faculties, and some administrators who will not support white teachers when they confront black students in their negative behaviors.

So one has to be careful and pick such battles wisely. And sometimes you may even have to back down. But when that happens the children and the country are not well served. Black children need teachers who will stand up to them and stand up for them.

Black children need teachers who will look beyond their faults and see their potentials. The classroom today is full of students who have special needs. They bring to the classroom a host of problems that the teacher has no control over. These problems may affect the students' performance in class and the attitude with which they come to class. Teachers must be careful not to let the problems that students have stifle their attempts to educate them.

Children who have faults also have potentials. Black children need teachers who will look beyond their faults and see their potentials. Educators are fault finders and fault fixers. I go to school looking for faults in children. I look for the faults that will keep them from living up to their potentials. I look for the faults so I can fix them and move the students toward the goals they seek. I know that behind every fault there is a need begging to be addressed.

Good teachers do not look at the faults and conclude that the child can not be helped; nor do they conclude that the faults define or limit the child. To an educator, a fault ought to inspire a rallying cry, not a surrender plea. A fault ought to be seen as a reason for our being. We should look beyond the fault and see the potential that can be realized if we overcome the fault.

Black children need teachers who believe that they can learn and who have a noble vision for them in today's society. Educators talk of high expectations, but people can only have high expectations for those whom they believe can live up to those expectations. There are many teachers who believe that black children can not meet high expectations and that those of us who are trying to raise them to such levels are simply wasting our time. Black students do not need teachers who think that way. Instead, they need teachers who think that they are capable of greatness and who have a plan to help them achieve that greatness. There are some of us in education who have been around long enough to remember when the reputation of black students was quite different from the reputation they have today. We remember black children who were well behaved, highly motivated, and passionate about learning. Consequently, we know what blacks can do when they apply themselves.

However, the younger class of educators might not have seen such blacks. They may have seen only the lazy, turned off kids who they have in their classes today. Therefore, they may have concluded that what they have is all there is, and that what the kids are producing is all that they are capable of producing. Unfortunately, it is up to those of us who know better to show better. Those of us who believe in the capabilities of black children are challenged to get those kids to excel and make believers out of the non believers. For in the end, black children will need teachers who believe that they can achieve excellence, and will push them until they do.

Finally black children need teachers who believe in the power of teachers, and further believe that against all odds a teacher can make a difference in a child's life. Black children need teachers who will use their power to help them build ladders rather than crutches, to look up rather than down, to climb mountains rather than dig ditches, to grow wings rather than to nurse scars, and who will help them be the very best human beings they can be.

Of Course, there are other things that black students need in their teachers. Their teachers need to be intelligent, well educated, patient, sensitive, kind, strict, organized, focused, and visionary, and the list goes on. What I have mentioned here are just a few things that the teachers of black children will need beyond those things if they are to be effective with black children today.

By now you may have concluded that these are qualities that all teachers should have in order to be effective teachers for any of our students today. You are exactly right. However, for some reason some teachers have been demonstrating these qualities when dealing with other students, but not when working with black students. The reason for this, in part, might simply be that black people have been placed in a special category and teachers have come to the conclusion that they are different. Part of the reason may be that dealing with black children has been too risky and most teachers don't want the hassle. Whatever the reason, black children need teachers who have these qualities. Black children are not going away. They will be in our public schools, and those teachers who teach in the public schools will have to teach them. The question is whether we will be effective teachers or whether we will simply go through the motions and send these kids out into the world as confused and as ignorant as we found them.

Tips On Teaching African American Children

1. **Always have high expectations**. Look up to the stars, not down at the tombs. The challenges blacks face will require the very best from them. The best thing teachers can do to help black children meet these challenges is to demand excellence in the classroom.

2. **Promote education as a Cure all**. Education is the key to much of what is wrong with black people. Befriend them if you will, sympathize with them if you must, but teach them whenever you can.

3. **Don't hesitate to call home.** Challenge black parents to get involved in the education of their children. Give them a chance to show their concern.

4. **Lead, don't Follow.** Stay in charge of your class and let students know that you are in charge. They are in school to learn from the teachers, not the other way around.

5. **Don't make or entertain excuses for black people's failures.** Black people are not the only ones who have had to overcome hardship to succeed. The road to success is paved with obstacles. Winners overcome obstacles.

6. **Conspire to educate black children.** Organize among yourselves and speak as one in making academic demands and enforcing school policies.

7. **Don't insist on over night success.** At-risk black children did not get to be the way they are in a day or a semester, and teachers will not be able to change them instantly. Often, progress in made long before the teacher sees it.

8. **Don't get caught up in endless discussions about race.** Periodic honest and open discussions about race are very helpful, but endless talk about such things at the expense of the curriculum are detrimental to black children.

9. **White teachers; don't spend valuable teaching time trying to convince black children that you are not a racist.** The most racist thing you can do to a black child is to allow him to remain ignorant.

10. **Be yourself.** Don't try to pretend with children. They can usually see through a fake. If you like children and want to help them, be yourself and teach them. **Whatever works best for you, do it!**

BOOK ORDER FORM

Understanding And Educating African-American Children

Date_____ __

purchase order No._____

Vendor's T.I.N 43-1672159   ISBN-1-884594-28-8

Price per single copy...$20.00

Five or more copies...$15.00 each

Shipping (single copy)..$ 3.25

Shipping (two copies)...$ 5.00

(Estimate shipping cost when ordering more than two copies.) _____

Amount Enclosed.._____

Amount Due.._____

Name   _____

Address_____ _____

_____ _____

_____ _____

Telephone_____FAX_____

DOCUMENTS ORDERED WITH THIS FORM ARE COPYRIGHTED AND ARE PROTECTED
BY COPYRIGHT LAW. DUPLICATION WITHOUT WRITTEN PERMISSION FROM
WILLIAM JENKINS IS PROHIBITED. MAKE CHECKS AND/OR MONEY ORDERS
PAYABLE TO:

WILLIAM   JENKINS ENT.
P. O. BOX 15134
ST. LOUIS, MO 63110
PH. (314) 652-7933
FAX (314) 533-1850

Visit our web site for more information about BOOKS, TAPES, Workshops, and
LECTURES. http://jenkins.freehosting.net/   E-Mial: wisdom@mo.net.

OTHER PUBLICATIONS

<u>A STUDENT'S GUIDE TO SUCCESS IN SCHOOL</u> is handbook on student success. It is a clear, down to earth, talk with students about the behaviors that lead to success and the behaviors that lead to failure. It is written in language that students as early as sixth grade can understand.

<u>A BLACK STUDENT'S GUIDE TO SUCCESS AT PREDOMINANTLY WHITE SCHOOLS</u> is a handbook for black students attending predominantly white schools. This brochure contains good information for any student, it will be particularly helpful to black students at predominantly white schools.

<u>THE A B C'S OF SEX</u> is a brochure about sex and the young person. It talks openly and honestly about sex, aids, pregnancy, and careers. It is neither religious nor moralistic, but a plain, common sense talk to teens about sex. This is the kind of information a student and his or her parents can discuss together.

<u>THE YOUNG AMERICAN'S GUIDE TO SUCCESS</u> is a brochure about being successful in America. This brochure is not just about school, but the things that every child should leave school knowing.

<u>PARENTING TOWARD SCHOOL SUCCESS</u> is a practical guide for parents on what to do to help children become successful school. It is great information that is easy to read and apply.
<u>A LITTLE BOOK FOR BIG PEOPLE</u>
An inspirational book for people of all races and engages. This book will warm your heart and make you feel good about life

<u>CHARACTER AND VALUES</u> is a character building and values teaching guide.

For information about, or to order any of these publications, address your inquiries to:

William Jenkins Ent.
P. O. Box 15134
St. Louis, MO 63110
Ph. (314) 652-7933
FAX (314) 5331850
E-mail: Wisdom@mo.net

A BLACK AMERICAN EMBRACES AMERICA
by William L. Jenkins

I shall not look to Africa Anymore, not for a home.
I shall not claim her as mine, for she does not desire me.
If I persist in claiming her against her will
I may lose my rightful place in this place, And rightfully so.
My hollow cries for a distant land are futile and empty.
America is my place, America is my home.
My ancestors, here against their will,
Willed to be here beyond their willed captivity.
They poured their blood, sweat, and tears into a common stream
So that they with others in this land could rightfully call themselves Americans.
I descended from their blood.
I inherited the liberty purchased with their blood, sweat, and tears.
This is the country God gave to my ancestors, and through them, to me.
I shall not challenge his providence, question his wisdom, nor reject his gift.
So I claim this land as mine.
Some can exist content in the nowhere between somewheres.
But I can not.
I need a place. I need a land.
I need a land to be from, a land to belong to,
A land to cling to, a land to return to, and a land to be loyal to.
America is my land by double choice: her of me and me of her.
This blood stained, fruited plain is mine.
My ancestors, friends and kinsmen lie buried beneath her soil
waiting for me to join them in eternity,
Nowhere else could I rest in peace. This is my country.
This America, my America.

BLACKNESS

I awoke this morning feeling very tired of being black.
I feel that way sometimes.
"How can that be?" you may ask.
Blackness is not a tiring condition.
Blackness is merely a color, like white, or yellow or green.
Oh no, you don't understand.
Blackness is much more than a color for those who are truly black.
Blackness is a condition.
Blackness is waking up every morning to news of the killings of your kind.
Blackness is the shame of bearing the burden for all that is bad.
Blackness is always having to be better just to be good enough.
No, that's not quite accurate.
Blackness is never being quite good enough.
So you can see why sometimes I tire of blackness.
I'm tired of drive by shootings and gang violence.
I'm tired of knowing that I have no value,
That if I were found dead in my yard in the morning,
"Drug related" is the only explanation that would be given.
I'm tired of being black: of talking black, eating black, and dying black.
I'm tired of singing black, and dancing black, and loving black.
I'm tired of feeling black, and touching black, and hugging black.
I'm tired of knowing that some blacks made me tired of black.
They say that black is beautiful.
Pain is not beautiful!
To be black is to be in constant pain.
Sometimes I grow tired of the pain.
Maybe that's it.
I'm not really tired of being black.
Maybe I'm just tired of blackness being pain.
Anyway, I'll feel better tomorrow.

William L. Jenkins